AFTERLIFE

Audrey Healy

Afterlife
Stories of After-Death Communication

CURRACH
PRESS

First edition, 2013, published by
CURRACH PRESS
55A Spruce Avenue, Stillorgan Industrial Park,
Blackrock, Co. Dublin

Cover design by Shaun Gallagher
Origination by Currach Press
Printed by Bell & Bain Ltd

ISBN 978 1 85607 806 1

Acknowledgements

I would like to thank the following people who assisted me in the compilation and publication of this book.

Author, friend and colleague Don Mullan, with whom I wrote *Contacted*, the first book on this subject, in 2005. Everyone who contributed the testimonies to this publication. I am very grateful to those who have shared their personal experiences in the hope that they might help each other. I would also like to thank Amanda Roberts, psychic medium, Anne Alcock, psychotherapist and spiritual director, Sr Mary Mullins, bereavement counsellor, historian Shane McCorristine, Bill Guggenheim, ADC Project, USA, 'Anchor' and 'Jackie', spiritual consultants, Barbara Mallon, psychic, and Sean Sugrue, psychotherapist.

I would also like to thank Fearghal, Patrick, Shane, Leeann, Valerie and all the staff at Currach Press, whom I have worked with before and who have been very enjoyable to work with. My thanks to the many newspapers and magazines, both national and provincial, who have publicised my appeal for testimonies; your support is much appreciated, particularly Shannonside Radio, the *Roscommon People*, *Longford Leader*, *Leitrim Observer*, *Roscommon Herald*, *Westmeath Topic*, *Athlone Advertiser* and *Westmeath Independent*.

Finally to James Wims, County Longford Librarian, Mary Carletron Reynolds, and all the staff of Longford Library for their kindness and support and to Irish Times Religious Affairs Correspondent Patsy McGarry for launching the book. I am very happy to have him involved and was very impressed by his contribution to one of my previous books, *The Rose and the Thorn*.

Finally, thank you to my parents, family and many friends for their ongoing support.

Audrey Healy
October, 2013

Contents

'Promise me you'll always remember: You're braver than you believe, and stronger than you seem, and smarter than you think.'

A. A. Milne

'Memories are better than diamonds and nobody can steal them away from you.'

Rodman Philbrick

Introduction

'I smiled back at her, and from that moment I felt peaceful and happy.' This is the kind of statement I regularly heard from people I met on my journey when I decided to compile this book on the fascinating subject of after-death communication. The subject of the living trying to communicate with the dead, through psychics and mediums, has been explored extensively in different ways. However, the testimonies in this compilation tell of spontaneous communication from the deceased to the living, a phenomenon known as after-death communication.

But does such a phenomenon really exist or is it all in the mind of the grief-stricken left behind? Have those who have gone before us gone forever or can they really communicate with us in some way? The majority of the contributors to this book from their experiences believe that those who have passed on try to reach out to us in our moments of sadness, to console us, and to tell us they are alright and at peace.

Following on from my first book on this subject, *Contacted*, co-written with Don Mullan in 2005, I continued to received letters and testimonies from people all over the world sharing their stories of after-death communication, some of them so gripping that I felt they warranted another collection.

The stories in this collection are diverse and varied. They are told by parents who have lost a child and feel their presence still, children who have lost beloved parents and grandparents, and ordinary people like you and I who understand the circle of life and accept that death is a part of it.

This book confronts the eternal question: *is death the end?* Nobody truly knows the answer to that question definitively, of course. Birth, death and grief are inevitable parts of life and parting is something we must all cope with at some stage of our lives. How we deal with it is an individual and very personal thing. Each one of us has lost someone close in our lives; but for many, they do not see death as the end, instead they believe in heaven and an afterlife; others go further, believing that those who have passed on can communicate with those left behind. Throughout the testimonies in this compilation we hear the convincing voice of those who have experienced what they perceive to be some form of after-death communication, whereby they have lost someone close to them, be it their mother, father, sibling, or close friend and have thereafter experienced an incident or event that has made them feel that that person is still with them.

Some people report hearing a voice and having an actual conversation with the deceased, similar to one they would have had with them in life. A significant number of people speak of smelling a fragrance; many told of the lingering aroma of their late mother's perfume of their late father's cigarette smoke. Similar common smells were the scent of flowers, in particular roses. Others describe sensing a presence, a distinct feeling that their loved one is nearby, even though he or she can't be seen or heard. Some talk of feeling a physical touch, a hand upon their shoulder, a pat on their back, all reassuring and comforting forms of contact.

A lot of people contacted me with experiences of dreams about their deceased loved one. They described graphic and very real conversations with relatives which stayed with them long after they had woken up.

Premonitions were another interesting factor in this book. A lot of people wrote of waking up in the night suddenly with thoughts of a close relative or friend only to be informed in the morning to that that person had in fact died at that precise time.

Ghosts also made their presence known in this compilation. We heard stories of people appearing out of nowhere and then disappearing into thin air, lights turning themselves on and off and duvet covers moving across sleeping bodies. Scary stuff!

However, the most amazing and convincing experiences shared with me are the visual experiences. They are so graphic and real that I believe they could not have come from anyone's mind, no matter how imaginative they can be. Whether I believe them or not does not really matter; what matters is that they are real to those who have experienced them. Appearances ranged in the testimonies from a ghostly transparent image to a full-bodied person similar to how the person in question was in life. Most looked well and radiant, despite the fact that some had been ill prior to death.

They spoke of love and reassured their relative here that they were well and happy.

It is easy to get caught up in the sentimentality of the testimonies, which are understandably extremely emotionally charged and moving. Because of this I felt it was beneficial to get the views of professionals who work in this area, experts who deal with the subject on a regular basis. I have included interviews with Amanda Roberts, psychic medium, Anne Alcock, psychotherapist and spiritual director, Sr Mary Mullins, bereavement counsellor, and historian Shane McCorristine, who holds a PhD in the supernatural, amongst others. These interviews are important and provide the valuable insight of professionals, some of whom have devoted their lives to after-death communication.

Having read such personal and heartfelt testimonies, am I any closer to discovering the truth? Probably not. But I truly believe that if the incidents recounted in this book bring hope and comfort to those who experienced them first-hand then they are valid and significant and worthy of documentation.

I hope that the expert opinions of the professionals interviewed may help you make up your own mind, but most of all it is my I hope that those who have experienced such an occurrence may find comfort in reading other people's stories.

1

What the Experts Say

Bill Guggenheim, ADC Project, USA

In the US, Bill Guggenheim, who serves on the Board of Advisors of the International Association for Near-Death Studies (IANDS), and Judy Guggenheim, interviewed two thousand people who reside in all fifty American states and the ten Canadian provinces who claim to have experienced after-death communication. Together they collected more than three thousand three hundred first-hand accounts from people who believe they have been contacted by a loved one who had died.

What they called the ADC project, was created in May 1988 to conduct the first in-depth research of After-Death Communications.

Judy and Bill and their ADC research have been featured on television, radio programs, and in numerous newspaper and magazine articles throughout the United States, Canada, and Europe.

'The majority of after-death communication events reported seemed to offer solace and peace to those who are grieving and in emotional pain. Therefore, there seems to be no harm in the phenomenon as long as it does not become an obsession or impact on your life in some way. Of course not everyone who has lost someone experiences contact and we can have no answers as to why this is but we hope you will find hope and comfort in reading other people's testimonies if you are grieving for someone in your life.'

Amanda Roberts, Psychic Medium and Healer, London

Amanda Roberts is a healer and psychic medium based at the College of Psychic Studies in South Kensington, London. She claims to remove negative energies, thought forms, spirit attachments, cords and contracts. She is also a psychic medium who teaches a variety of spiritual and healing workshops and a teacher and consultant of Spiritual Response Therapy.

Roberts says that people from all different walks of life appear to have experienced varying degrees of such communication, although they are primarily female. 'People come from a wide variety of cultural and ethnic backgrounds,' she tells me.

'It is mainly woman who come to see me and due to where I am based at the moment the majority come from higher socio-economic groups. When I was working as a medium in the spiritualist churches more men and those from lower socio-economic groups would also be present.'

Amanda initially decided to become a healer prior to training as a medium, which she describes as 'the best thing I did, as it taught me how to communicate clearly with those who had passed over who had being coming through to me.'

Her decision to choose this career path was very much influenced by her own experiences which she has shared with me. 'I have had a number of personal experiences through the years – in that those who came through were people who I knew who had died. I have experienced a lot of death in my life and a number of those who I knew come through from time to time. It is often just about being present and as with my sitters I find this very comforting.'

'I know when my dad comes through as there is a smell of cigarette smoke around. He was a keen smoker until about ten years before he died and I guess that is a very easy way for me to identify when he is with me. When my mum was dying she came through and waved goodbye to me before she died, as a way of telling me she was going. I live in England and she lived in New Zealand. She waited for me to get back before she died but at that stage she was moving in and out of awareness – people can often come through in these situations.'

Many of the people who approach Amanda for assistance, she says, are actively attempting to contact the deceased, although some are just simply living with the awareness of a physical and emotional presence, similar to many of those who have written to me for this compilation. 'When they visit me they want me to contact their deceased ones to bring through messages for them. A lot of them are aware of their deceased ones being around them. This offers them comfort but while they are aware of them being around them they are generally unable to get messages from them for themselves.'

'What I do now is help people to deal with grief and loss so that they can move on with their lives. The other part of what I do is coming through with clear life paths or choices that can also help them move on in their lives.'

As so many of the contributors in this book have found, there is such a diverse range of contact, from actual visions, to dreams, to sounds, premonitions and what could be simply perceived as coincidence – and Amanda has come across them all in her profession. 'The most common form of contact for my clients is knowing or sensing the presence of a loved one around them at particular times.'

Other ways can be things being left or found such as coins, things being moved which they associate with the person, a smell, dreams, robins being in the vicinity (actual birds). 'Sometimes people can see them either in their mind's eye or they may appear as a physical being to them. Some people can also hear them.'

The passing of a loved one can leave many practical as well as emotional difficulties and ultimately many unanswered questions. In her work Amanda hopes she can be of some help to those left behind. 'Death is messy in that it often leaves lots of loose ends,' she points out. 'Mistresses, for example, may turn up at funerals and wives and children want answers as to what was going on or happening. This can help to answer questions and to assist the sitter to release their anger in situations like that. Other people commit suicide, leaving many unanswered questions and a very deep grief for friends and family, especially when it involves a young person.'

'People can die violently, suddenly and in totally unexpected situations. There is often fear that the person may be stuck and not have passed over. If that is the case I can assist them over,' she says. 'This can happen in sudden death as people may not be aware that they have died, which is where ghosts come in. When there has been a long serious illness people want reassurance that their loved ones have passed over and are happy on the other side.'

For those who are lost and grieving, Amanda hopes she can offer some kind of solace and perhaps some hope that their loved one is still with them and happy. 'When someone comes for a sitting I explain what mediumship is to ensure they know it is contacting those that have passed over. I then say they cannot come with a shopping list, as if someone is not ready to come through then it will not happen,' she explains.

'I then close my eyes and ask for anyone who has passed over who has a message that is relevant, practical and specific to please come through. I get the deceased person's personalities, what they look like, their build, and then come through with the relevant messages for the client.'

She believes that those who are still here are often looking for guidance and advice from those who have gone before us. 'Sitters often are looking for answers or confirmation as to choices that are relevant in their life at the time of the sitting. They can often be facing challenges and they want their loved one to still assist them and advise them from the other side.'

Amanda is of the opinion that while people often become emotional during the sitting, generally it is a time of great comfort and joy. 'Questions get answered, people find out that their deceased one is happy on the other side and advice that is relevant to situations in the person's present life gets answered. People often leave feeling a lot happier and lighter than when they arrived.'

Anne Alcock, Psychotherapist, Life Coach and Spiritual Director, Cork

County Cork based Anne Alcock describes herself as 'a Roman Catholic who works within the Christian tradition'. As a psychotherapist, life coach and spiritual director she offers spiritual direction within the Catholic tradition. 'Many people have lost loved ones and in my experience what they bring to the session is the fact of death and their experience of coping with the loss. Implicit in this, being Christian, is that this is not the end and the person will be now with God.'

'As a Christian I believe in eternal life and that those who have died live on in some way. I would be open to the possibility of the dead being 'present in some sense', in the same way that I am open to the reality of the presence of God.'

However, only sometimes have people mentioned after-death communication to Anne. 'Very occasionally someone might say, I pray to her, I do talk to her, but they have not mentioned any sense of presence in the sense I understand you to mean it.'

Anne says that people 'seem content in their faith that their loved one is at peace'. 'It is more that they would hope to meet them after death on the other side rather than any concern, expectation or experience than the loved one would be revisiting this side. I only remember this being talked about in Africa, as a child, but only in the context of dark spirits and witchcraft.'

People go through many difference stages of grief says Anne. 'In the first shock of bereavement many people experience the stages of grief outlined by Elizabeth Kubler Ross and others, which include numbness and denial and anger so sometimes it is impossible to pray because the anger is directed at God so often a person can't pray, feels cut off, lost. Later on the belief of God and the idea of a place of rest for the loved one becomes easier to take in and provides some comfort. So in my experience, prayer before the death and prayer at a time after the death is more likely than prayer immediately after the death. However the rituals of prayer do provide a context in which to go through the grieving process and it also depends on what is meant by "prayer".'

Anne concludes by saying that grief is very personal. 'It is a process. I have heard people tell of their irritation when they recount well meaning clichés like *it was for the best* or *she'll be happier now*. So myself, I say very little. I make myself available to listen. I try and support by empathy, calm and in this case a herbal tea! The life eternal is a mutual assumption; the sadness is with people here coming to terms in this life.'

Sean Sugrue, Psychotherapist, Dublin

Dublin based psychic medium and psychotherapist Sean Sugrue believes that we all have the ability to contact the deceased and that people are actually seeking contact, particularly in these challenging economic times. 'People are looking for a connection and they do sense their deceased loved ones around them in some way.' This phenomenon is, states Sean, one that covers all spectrums. 'People from all different walks of life and different occupations come to me for help,' he says, 'and I teach people to communicate as well. I do a bit of mediation and act as a medium between us and the spirit world and I try to open up that connection between people.'

'I believe that you're not just a human being, you're a spiritual being and you have to live in the spiritual as well as the physical.'

'We all have the ability to connect with our loved ones and it's getting all more evident today. We are more sensitive to it,' Sean continues. 'All religions ultimately believe in the one thing and the way things are with the Catholic Church people are questioning things a lot. In the past we did what we are told and we are now opening up to all these things.'

So, how does communication between those who have passed and the living actually work on a practical level? Quite simply Sean says that the basis of it is the love between the living and the dead. 'I believe if you went up to someone and they ignored you, after a while you would get pissed off and you would back away and it's the same with the spirit world. If they [the deceased] are trying to contact you and you ignore them, they will back away but they will still be there and I believe that the basis of that is love and when we pass into the spirit world that love never dies. When we pass into that world God himself is not going to stop you coming back and communicating with those who loved you.'

So is such communication messing with the supernatural or is it simply maintaining a relationship with those loved ones who went before? Can it be dangerous? Or is it bringing joy and solace to those who are grieving? Sean has his own thoughts. 'People get a lot of comfort from this regardless of what religion they believe in. I have had people from all religions come to me, as well as walks of life. They have all experienced this and it helps them through their pain.'

So what brought Sean down this road? Was it a career choice or something deeper? 'It was definitely a calling for me because I saw Our Lady when I was four or five years of age,' reveals Sean. 'I was a carpenter by trade but then I had had a few different experiences throughout my life. It was a stepping stone for me.'

It's a controversial topic and for those of us who are tentative about opening up our hearts and our minds to communications can we engage in it? To a certain degree, says Sean. 'It's up to everyone if they open themselves up to it,' he says. 'If they are putting up a barrier, it's as I said earlier, if someone is putting up an obstacle and someone is ignoring them, after a while they will get pissed off. I currently do house parties and there would be seventeen or eighteen people there and usually within that group there would be a few skeptics there but I'm not there to change anyone's point of view. I'm just there to provide a medium for communication.'

'Anchor' and 'Jackie', Spiritual Consultants, USA

Husband and wife duo 'Anchor' and 'Jackie' from the US spoke to me about their experiences as spiritual consultants in the US, where they run an organisation called Afterlife 101.

Jackie says her unique spiritual experiences began when she was just a child. 'My personal experience talking to the other side, began when I was an infant,' she explains. 'A lady who lived in our apartment had died there and was like my personal guard and friend straight from heaven, so I have always spoke to the other side. As I grew older and had such communications with angels and spirit guides I agreed to be a channel for those on the other side and have been doing so for over sixty years.'

Jackie says she does not find such contact intrusive but says sometimes people here on earth simply cannot let go of their loved ones. Many people come to her for help in contacting them.

'Yes, people do come to me wanting to speak with those on the other side. I do not just go up to someone and tell them a departed loved one wants to talk with them unless it is someone I know very well. I like being with someone personally when we can communicate with the other side but I can also do this over the phone.'

'I haven't ever found this to be intrusive by the spirits, but several times by people here on earth who cannot let go of their loved ones.'

'Many people think either the spirit or myself are psychic and often are looking for answers to living their lives. That is something I try to stay away from unless the spirit has something very important to tell them.'

And are they typically afraid or comforted by such contact?

'Rarely do I have someone who is afraid and asks to discontinue but it has happened and they have always come back and want to finish.'

Jackie claims spirits contact her 'because I have agreed to be a channel needed on earth to share this most loving act and to help humans not to be afraid of death ... that life does continue.'

For those who simply do not believe in after-death communication she says, 'Sometimes one of their personal loved ones will jump in with a message for me to tell them something that I have no way of knowing. Sometimes nothing happens at all and I know they just aren't ready for opening that part of themselves. I honour that and let it go.'

Jackie says she loves being able to experience the gifts that she has been given, both for herself and for the others who come and ask to speak with departed loved ones. She does not charge any fees for her services this but asks for the people to kindly contribute something to an animal shelter.

'I honor and respect my many gifts I have been given. My life is based on knowing and loving God,' she concludes.

Jackie says that she and her husband, Anchor, have remained largely anonymous for all these years for professional reasons: 'Because of the positions my husband held while spending twenty-eight years in the navy and eighteen years after that while in the high security private industry. There are still so many who do not believe who could cause us much trouble.'

Jackie's husband, Anchor, says he has not really had any personal experiences himself. Rather, he says, 'My personal experiences do not stem from any spiritual gift that I may have. Instead, they take place primarily due to exposure to the words coming from my wife when she is in a trance and the spirit coming through having an interactive conversation with me. I also have had the experience of being in the audience when professional mediums perform.'

Anchor says that the nature of the spiritual experience is always peaceful, since it takes place upon request.

'People come to my wife from sources who learn of her gifts through her or her friends and my experience is that people who have sessions with my wife are almost always comforted by that experience.'

He believes that spirits contact him 'at such times that my wife is in trance and generally because of my request to speak with them. I believe that our spirit guides are motivated by a concern for our well-being and have extensive telepathic conversation with my wife during her day, without her being in a trance mode.'

As previously referred to, Anchor says that he and his wife have specific reasons for remaining anonymous.

'I summarise this in the forward to the Afterlife 101 PDF book. My work and school experience, now spanning over sixty years, and involving senior positions in the navy and in the aerospace industry did not bring me in contact with many individuals whom I believe share my spiritual beliefs. I see very little advantage in open disclosure of these beliefs as opposed to the disadvantage from sceptical comments I would receive from the mass of my military and civilian friends. In addition, I live in an area of America, the Missouri Ozarks, that is heavily Baptist oriented and we would not like to become isolated by our nearby acquaintances as kooks and anti-Christian people. We do, however, participate periodically in groups of local individuals who do share in our spiritual beliefs – and UFO beliefs as well – and who preserve our anonymity.'

For those interested in more information on Afterlife 101 Anchor refers you to *afterlifedata.com*, 'which is an extensive comparison of the findings of the Afterlife 101 book with over eight hundred extracts from other spiritual sources. We found that there was about ninety-five per cent agreement with what our spirit guides stated and the other source extracts.'

Sr Mary Mullins, Bereavement Counsellor, Dublin

Sr Mary Mullins, who works with those who have been bereaved, says that many of the people she has dealt with 'have a strong sense of their loved ones being present to them, they feel this intuitively. They feel their loved one is caring for them, protecting them from danger, helping them with decisions. This sense can be very strong for some people, for example if the person escapes uninjured in an accident they will say the deceased was looking after them. This is very comforting and helps the person cope with the loss.'

Throughout this book we see that many examples of after-death communication involve dreams. Sr Mary too says, 'Many people dream about their dead loved one. This is comforting but also upsetting afterwards because the loved one is no longer present. Some people feel something while they are in bed at night. Being touched by someone or seeing the shape of someone. Often people see white butterflies and see this as a sign from their loved one that they are present.'

Sr Mary adds that many people find counselling very helpful in dealing with their grief because they can talk about the details of the death, the funeral, and the loss. Crying in the presence of somebody else is healing and helps the bereavement process. 'Prayer too is very important for some people. It is a real resource for those who believe in God; lighting candles, visiting the grave, flowers, preparing for anniversaries, rituals, etc.'

As for the practice of mediumship, Sr Mary takes a more wary view. 'Some people receive messages through mediums, sometimes there is a genuine connection through someone, but sometimes it is not good and can be dangerous and damaging.'

Barbara Mallon, Psychic, Virginia, USA

Barbara Mallon is a psychic medium based in Manassas, Virginia, USA and says that people from all different spectrums come to her for help.

'Most who want a session with me are looking to hear if their passed loved one is ok and at peace. By receiving evidential pieces of information from the spirit people, they are able to see that indeed they are ok and that they really aren't dead. They are still around and see what we're up to, etc. Most have had visits from their spirit people and sometimes this is even validated in the session.'

Barbara says that the most common forms of contact reported are through dreams, feeling the presence of their loved one, and smelling perfumes or cigarette smoke, etc.

In her professional capacity Barbara, who has had some personal experiences of communication herself, says she loves to give the spirit people the chance to let their loved ones know they are ok and also to relay messages. She adds, 'I ask the spirit person for evidential pieces of information which will help to identify who they are to my client and then any messages they wish to convey. Mediumship should never take the place of grief counselling or counselling of any kind, but it can be very healing to hear from a passed loved one.'

In Barbara's opinion, in the majority of cases – though not all – such contact will offer comfort and reassurance to those in grief. 'Nine times out of ten a session will comfort clients, but sometimes it can be difficult to feel the "essence" of a spirit person again and it can be bittersweet,' she explains. 'It never upsets a client, but sometimes clients will become upset if they don't hear from whom they wish to (anyone may come through), so that can be a little tough, but this is why I always say to leave expectations at the door and expect anyone. Spirits always know best what we need to hear.'

2

Visions

This chapter deals with instances where grieving friends or family members experience visitations from or apparitions of their deceased loved ones. It contains moving and graphic stories in which people experience the love and tenderness of their loved ones who have passed on. For the most part these visions brought comfort, reassurance and hope.

Barbara, USA
When I was in high school, my grandfather passed away just before my graduation. He lived with us for years before we had to put him into a nursing home because he had a stroke. My mom just had a baby in 1969 and my father put his back out picking up my grandfather in the bathroom where he fell. He was upset that we could not keep him in our home anymore, so I used to visit him daily after school.

I went to see him in April with my Italian girlfriend who would translate for me when he went back to speaking his language. I told him not to be upset; we would take him to our house for Easter and be with the family. He said, 'I will not be here. Noni came to see me and wants me with her.' I was very upset that he was suggesting he would die and be with his wife and not with us. We were very close. Well, as he predicted, he died of heart failure on Good Friday and never came to our home for Easter.

He was a very religious man. I slept in his old room for months with his pictures and statues of Mother Mary and kept his rosary beads with me. At his funeral and wake I was so upset that instead of crying I laughed. I couldn't control it. I had never had anyone I loved so much die and my emotions were everywhere. My other grandmothers had died when I was very young, so I don't think I really understood what death was until his.

One night, a few weeks after he died, I was going to bed in his room and he appeared to me, at the end of the bed, in front of his religious shrine, and told me that it was okay and he was sorry to leave us, but he wanted to be with Noni and now he was and he was very happy. He told me to tell my mother that they were happy together now. He was as real as if he were standing there alive. He said it was ok that I laughed; he knew I meant to cry. He was gone as fast as he appeared, but I never forgot the moment. I was not scared. I was awake. I knew he loved me and came back to tell me and my mom he was okay and knew we missed him and he loved us but was not happy since he lost his wife and now he was with her. It was 1974.

That was my first experience actually seeing someone.

This was my next experience. I was engaged to a biker, Al, that no one in my family liked, but I loved. We dated and lived together since 1974. I always felt safe with him. He got involved with some bad people and I broke up with him after asking him to please move to California with me to change his life, but he refused. I moved in August 1979. I then received a phone call from my girlfriend who said he had been killed on January 13, 1980 by the people he was involved with. I did not have enough money to go back to his wake and funeral, so my friend went in my place. I lit candles for him and cried for days. I had just moved into an apartment by myself for the first time. I was scared every night and missed him beside me.

One night, while I was sitting up in the living room, afraid to go to sleep, he appeared and sat next to me. He said not to worry, ever. He was watching over me and would make sure nothing bad would ever happen to me. He told me that even if I couldn't see him or feel him, that he was always there and not to be afraid. He would take care of me from somewhere else and I would always be loved. He left and I have never seen him again, but have sometimes felt him and remembered his words that comforted me for years.

I never thought I could love again, but I did. In 1984, I met a man named Bob, my dad's name. We dated for six years, long distance from Massachusetts to New Jersey. I felt like I had Al's blessing and was happy until 1990. He asked me to marry him. I declined because I wanted to go back to California and he wouldn't move, and then there was an incident. We broke up and I flew back to California and lived there until 1994.

I was very close to my dad and we had a connection that my mom and I had never formed. In 1992, still in California, I had a dream that my dad had been dropped by two men and was bleeding and they had to take his shirt off and take him away. I called home very early the next morning only to find out he had had a heart attack and the EMTs almost dropped him going out the front door and he banged his arm on the moulding and was bleeding, so they took his shirt off to see how bad it was, wrapped it up and continued to the hospital. I asked my mom why she didn't call and tell me immediately and she said she didn't want me to worry as I was so far away and could do nothing about it. She was planning to call me when she knew he would be alright. I was very upset and told her that no matter how far away I was, I would always know when something was wrong and to please keep me informed so I wouldn't have these awful dreams anymore.

I moved home a couple of years later as my dad was ill. I lived with my parents and went back to school. My dad was very proud of me. For the next ten years he was in and out of the hospital I work at with a pacemaker, heart attack, stroke, dialysis, hip replacement, low blood pressure, etc. I was always by his side and slept at the hospital overnight when he was in, and went to work in my department at 7 a.m. I attached him to dialysis for years, every night, gave him daily shots, took his blood and cleaned him when he had accidents. I stopped my life to take care of him and don't regret one second of it.

The night he died, he was home and asked me to give him a haircut and a shave and a sponge bath. Then he said he didn't feel well and would like to go to the hospital. We all went up with him. I left at nine and my sister and mother were going to stay until eleven and then my brother was going to spend the night. We never left him alone in the hospital. I found out my brother went home on my mother's orders, so I called the nurses who said he wasn't doing well and went to the ICU. I raced to the hospital to be with him and stayed until 1 a.m. when he asked me to go home and get his glasses and teeth, which my mom had taken with her, so he could have breakfast and read the paper in the morning. This was our daily ritual.

I left to pick them up and get a few things. No sooner did I get home when the phone rang and they said he had died. I could not tell my mom he was dead, just said we had to get back to the hospital as soon as possible. It was a big mess trying to get there as they were in the middle of the Big Dig in Boston, the nightclubs were getting out at 2 a.m. and all the roads I knew were closed. It was a very stressful ride to the hospital. My siblings were also racing there from different cities. It was a terrible scene as they did not know he had died. They were distraught with grief and I was mad that the resident doctor did all the wrong things to save him because he had not read his chart.

After we got home and went to bed, I lay in my room wondering why I left him alone, I should have stayed. Maybe he would still be alive. All of a sudden, my door flew open and a breeze flew through the room, I heard, 'I'm free, I'm finally free!' I cried for his happiness and our loss but knew he was in a better place and free from all his pain.

A few hours later, my cousin called me from Connecticut. She asked if my dad was okay because she had just had a horrible dream and said he had been at her house. She quoted to me every detail of the night exactly as it happened and said she knew he had passed. I was sure then that we all have connections to the afterlife if we are open and aware.

He has come back several times on Sunday mornings, leaving a puddle of water in the kitchen on the floor where he used to get up, sing and make breakfast for us on his favourite day of the week. He comes to me at work in the supply room when I'm alone. The lights flicker and I know something is wrong, with me, my mom or my relatives. Every time it happens, I call my mom and the last three times, my aunt had just died, my uncle died and then my other uncle died.

There is a red cardinal that comes by and looks into my mom's kitchen window when she's at the sink. I'm pretty sure it's my dad watching over her still. Every now and then, the dog acts up and the cats hide and the lights flicker and fans go on and off. I think he is still trying to communicate with my mom and me.

Also, my dad used to give nickels to us when we did a good job. They show up in the strangest places now and no one knows how they got there. There was one in my new car when I bought it and on his car when we gave it to my niece and she came out of school, in the bathroom wall when it was being demolished to put in a shower for my mom and in the baseboard of my new kitchen when I was putting in a stove. We leave nickels on top of his grave when we go to see him.

His name was Robert Francis Lyons and his family is from Cork. I can still see his bright blue eyes and smiling face every time I think of him as if no time has passed. He died 9 November 2003 in Boston Massachusetts, where he was born 2 April 1923.

I had some interesting experiences in Ireland as well. One was in a castle that we were getting a private tour of. Many strange things happened and I found out later that the original owners of the castle years ago were part of my family. I didn't find out until we got home and my cousin, who has been researching our family tree, saw the name of an ancestor on the picture I took of the family tree that was on the wall of the castle.

Then last year, myself and a friend went down the old bog road in Athlone next to her father's house to see the some new calves. On the way back we tried to pick some chestnuts from an old tree on the side of the small road but the branch was too high, so she said we could come back with the tractor the next day. I sensed we were not alone and we hurried up the dark path where my friend's dad had his grandson waiting at the top to come looking for us as he also had sensed something was there. The next day we went back and the biggest branch of the tree had cracked in half and fallen across the road so no one could pass, but we could collect our chestnuts with ease now. My friend's dad said the tree was over three hundred years old and there was no wind or rain that night to cause the branch to fall. He said that the Potters did that for me. The Potters were a family who lived in a little stone cottage and were buried on the premises as they could not afford a real burial. He also said that many people have been spooked on that road and would not go there anymore. My friend would not go there alone since she was a girl as she heard some noises while picking vegetables for her mother and was spooked. She came with me only to show me the cows. Her brother and his son had to cut the tree and drag it away with trackers so the cows and farmers could pass and get to the other fields. I'll never forget it and neither will all her family. That happened in April 2009.

Karolina, County Offaly, Ireland
My name is Karolina. I live in County Offaly. I am a twenty-three year old Polish girl living in Ireland for about four years. On the 2 August 2008 my only brother died in a car accident and since that time I have been lucky enough to see him a few times. Most of the time I can talk to him when I am asleep, other times there's a specific smell, which everyone in a room can smell; but I have only seen him a few times. Most of the times when he had contacted me I wrote it in my diary. After the first contact I started searching the internet for things like this. I was a bit scared, but extremely happy. He knows when to come; when I need him most. I read a book called *Greetings from Heaven* which was a huge help and gave me hope.

Veronica, Manchester, UK
Things happen that can't be explained and in the past I have had a few. We had a much-loved dog, Lassie, who

died and one day I went to my mother's house and let myself in because my mother was out. I waited for an hour and decided she would be late so I wrote a note. Whilst I was doing this I became aware of a shadow and looking towards the kitchen I saw Lassie standing there, looking at me. She was solid and it seemed as though I could touch her. I spoke to her saying how upset we all were at her passing and all of a sudden she had gone. I had the feeling she had come back to see me. I never mentioned it to anyone as I felt they would have laughed. But I still think of her today just standing there.

A premonition is like having a daydream. One day I was washing up when I saw in my mind's eye my sister pass a window and knock on the door. She came to tell me that our father had died and I thought *what a silly thing to say!* even though Dad was in hospital at the time. Two days later, as I was having tea with my in-laws, that exact scene occurred just as I had foreseen it. It was uncanny. Dad had passed away with none of us there with him.

The day of the funeral was wet and cold. That night going to bed, I reached the top of the stairs when an overpowering smell of fresh flowers was all around. It lasted for all of ten minutes then faded away.

My husband was a home film-maker, always busy editing. One day he brought a Laurel Log that he had found in the cemetery after another funeral home and had the idea of using it for a logo because of our friend Stan Laurel. Every time he brought out the log it was greener and more plump, which was odd. As time went on it struck us, people we knew were dying and in that year we lost six souls, relations and friends. In the end the log was green; after twelve months it should have withered to some extent, not bloom like it did. It was decided to return it to the cemetery, which we did. After that we had less news, it was a relief.

Diana, County Galway, Ireland

I moved to Ireland twenty years ago from the UK. My mother was living in Yorkshire at the time. I received a telephone call one evening from my brother, informing me that my mum had suffered a brain haemorrhage. She was in intensive care and the outcome was not looking good for her. I flew over to the UK the following morning and sat at my mother's bedside at the hospital for hours, along with my sister and brother. My brother and sister decided to go to my sister's house for a rest and a meal for a couple of hours. Mum was non-responsive and I sat alone with her for an hour, then one of her friends arrived and sat with me. Mum was attached to monitors and the doctors had told us it was just a matter of time before she passed away.

Suddenly I heard the heart machine bleeping and the numbers on the machine started to go down, indicating that her heart was failing. The staff came in and said that Mum was passing away. Then I saw a golden shape lifting out of my mum's body – it rose up out of her, it was my mum! Her spirit or soul or whatever people would like to call it … I knew the staff and my mum's friend could not see this amazing sight. I stared at her and she lifted up out of her body and floated to the ceiling, looked down at me and smiled, then went through the ceiling of the room. She looked happy and at peace. My daughters and I have had so much contact with Mum since she passed away.

Joan, Manchester, UK
My story goes back a long way – ten years ago to be exact. My father had, at that time, been dead twenty years. I will start by saying what a truly devoted couple my mum and dad were. They met at just fifteen years of age, married at twenty-five and were completed devoted to each other. You never saw one without the other.

When I used to go and visit my mum after my father had died I used to think how sad and lonely she looked without him at her side. It didn't look right. It was as though she had lost part of her body.

After one of my many visits to my dear mum, I was leaving one day and as I turned to wave goodbye from the gate I was thinking how sad and lost she looked without my father at her side when all of a sudden all I can describe as a mist appeared above my mum's head, came down slowly and when it became level with Mum's shoulders it took the form of my father, not as a ghost but in the flesh and he was wearing what looked like a grey suit similar to one he used to wear.

The vision then vanished from sight and I never saw anything like it again. It was just as if my father had come back to tell me that my mum wasn't alone and that he was at her side looking after her as he always had. What a comfort that was to me! It is now thirty years since he died and my mum passed away almost seven years ago. I really do believe since seeing that vision that they are both reunited again and as happy in their afterlife as they were here on earth.

This brings me to the end and a very happy ending to my story 'I saw a vision.'

George, County Roscommon, Ireland
My mother was born and reared on a farm about three miles from Ballymote town. They lived in an old two-storey house that was previously owned by a man who had a reputation for being a joker as he played tricks on people whenever he got the chance. This man had died suddenly while working in a field below the house.

One evening when my mother was about ten and her brother was two years older, they were playing in the lawn in front of the house. Her mother called them and asked them to go and get the young donkey and put him in his stable for the night, as they did most nights except when their father did it. It was just beginning to get dark and their father was not home from the bog yet. When they looked down the field they saw the donkey about two hundred yards away. They got their long rods as usual and ran down the field towards where the donkey was grazing. When they got within fifty yards of the donkey her uncle told my mother to go down and turn the donkey up and that he would direct him towards the stable. My mother ran down and lifted her rod over the donkey with the intention of giving him a little tip to start him up the field.

The donkey disappeared into thin air right in front of her eyes!

The two children were very frightened and caught each other by the hand and ran for home and told their mother what had happened. When their mother checked the stable she found that the donkey had come in by himself some time earlier. They later discovered that the previous owner of the farm had dropped dead in the very same spot where the donkey disappeared.

George, County Roscommon, Ireland

While visiting my cousin in Seattle in 1999 I had occasion to pass through the kitchen early one morning when there was nobody in the house except my wife and I. The kitchen and sitting room was open plan, just divided by a fireplace and chimney with open archway at each side of the fireplace leading from the kitchen to the sitting room.

As I passed the first archway in the kitchen I saw my uncle, who had died two years previously, sitting on a sofa in the sitting room!

Despite being very frightened, I passed the fireplace and looked in through the other archway but there was nobody there. I hurried back to the bedroom where my wife was and told her what I had seen. I felt so shocked that my arms were covered with large goose pimples. I will never know did actually I see my dead uncle? Was it an illusion? Or was it my own mind playing tricks on me?

3

Voices

Testimonies in this chapter state that while deceased loved ones did not actually appear, they did, however, manifest themselves through whispered words or sounds that made the hearers aware of their presence. Remarkably, sometimes these sounds were heard across oceans, on the far side of the earth, and often before the hearer had been made aware of their loved one's death.

It is concluded by most who have experienced this that the deceased had come to say goodbye. This suggests that the dead are not gone, and in dying have been released from the limitations of time and space.

Mary Lou, Ontario, Canada

I was raised by my aunt and uncle and after my aunt passed away, I was driving on a country paved road one day and there was a side road coming up that was hidden in the one direction by a home built right on the corner. There was a stop sign in both directions for the side road, so I wasn't worried about it. All of a sudden, in my aunt's very clear voice, I heard her yell 'Stop!' and I hit the brakes. Right then a tractor pulling a wagon drove out onto the paved road. The poor man driving the tractor looked in my direction and I thought he was going to faint. I guess he couldn't see me coming because of the house either, but he didn't stop. He was waving and I could see him saying, 'I'm sorry', but fortunately nobody was hurt and no accident occurred. I have told the story to some people and know that some of them don't really believe me, as they just kind of smile. But I know what I heard.

My other story is that we lost our daughter Lisa to Cystic Fibrosis when she was forty-six years of age. That is actually quite old for that illness, as when she was diagnosed we were told she wouldn't live to be three years old. We were so fortunate to have her in our lives and loved her so very much. She married and had a daughter of her own, which we are eternally happy for. At her memorial service, her husband wanted to play a song from a CD that she loved. He said that she was always bopping around the house whenever she heard it.

I know many people felt it was inappropriate for the occasion, but we didn't care, Lisa loved the song. While it was playing, all of us (her family) in the front row of the many people present, noticed a large painting of her was swaying back and forth throughout the entire song. My husband, her father, always the sceptic, said that there was probably a breeze. We were all very quick to point out that not a petal or a leaf on any flower around the painting was moving.

After the service, many of our friends and relatives came back to our house. Many were in the basement around the bar and I was moving up and down trying to make sure everyone had everything they needed. While I was up in the kitchen, our other daughter said, 'Mom, tell them about Lisa's picture at the funeral home today.' I did so and all of a sudden, one of my best friends said, 'Oh my God, look at your chandelier in the dining room.' We all turned and looked, and sure enough, it was swinging back and forth. Just to be clear, there was no door or window open, or any reason for a very heavy iron chandelier to be moving. We know it was Lisa, saying goodbye and that she was enjoying everything about the day, especially the party. She had a wonderful sense of humour and would very much enjoy pulling these tricks on us, her loved ones.

Those are my stories and I hope you enjoy reading them, because it was nice for me to be able to write them.

Irene, UK

My mother died in 1989. I was sitting at home feeling numb when I heard these words in my head: 'Don't worry, I am alright.'

From then on until the funeral, I felt as if I wrapped in a comfort blanket.

Patricia, Louth, Ireland

In the early hours of the 5 June 2005 my father, a farmer and a man of nature, lay dying in the room I am now writing in. Although he did not believe in life after death he had accepted his death as he believed he would not get better from his illness. My three sisters and I were by his side. My father had a terrible struggle trying to die.

As time went by only myself and another sister were in the room. As we sat there quietly, one each side of his bed, a voice broke through from the other side. This perfectly audible voice seemed to emanate from the wall at the right hand side of my father's head where I was sitting. The voice was beautiful. It was a female voice with an even tone. However, its language I did not understand, it sounded Latin, although it has been suggested it may have been Sanskrit. The voice lasted for two to three minutes. I did not feel afraid, I felt privileged.

Later, I felt like telling the world, I actually felt this revelation should be on the six o'clock news. I wanted to reassure everybody there is life after death. I felt relieved for my father when his soul finally left his body, and, although it may sound cold-hearted, I did not feel the need to shed a tear, I knew he had been met on his journey and was now safe with his loved ones.

The day following his funeral I visited his grave to admire all the lovely flowers people had brought. When I got back into my car the smell of soggy burnt embers seemed to have filled it. When I reached home I decided to rest for a while only to discover I could still smell the smoke, even though I was no longer in my car but in my bed.

Quite some time later I by chance heard Liam Lawton, the singer, introduce a song on TV. As he did so he said the smell of burning embers are the sign of an angel!

4

Unexplained Paranormal Experiences

Here, several people tell their stories of paranormal experiences, strange and unexplained sounds and sightings that occurred in their lives. In some cases these experiences are unwelcome and frightening events; in other cases they are interpreted as comforting contact from deceased family members and friends.

If what these testimonies say is to be believed, it appears that the dead are not gone forever and exist in another realm and form. Judge for yourselves.

Joe, UK

I had this experience a number of years ago. I was living on my own at the time. I had a small experience in my own room where I felt a flutter or a wave across the duvet. I jumped up and wondered *what was that?* I thought I was dreaming so I shrugged it off and moved to a room downstairs.

A month later the same thing happened but when I went to move I was seized as if somebody had put their two arms around me. I was completely stuck and couldn't shout. I was told it wasn't trying to hurt me but at this stage I was scared shitless. This voice I heard was not like we speak but in my head. I managed to say 'fuck off' and it left me immediately. It frightened the hell out of me and I slept in the sitting room for a month or so with the lights on.

Diane, Spain
I feel I have to tell you about my brother. I received a phone call on Wednesday 19 May 2010 to say he had been admitted to hospital that morning but not to worry as they thought it was just kidney stones. As my husband and I live in Spain we were informed it was nothing too serious but the next day we decided to go to the UK and booked the earliest flight, which was Friday the 21st. Then we received another call Thursday night to say that my brother wasn't going to make it.

We got a call at 1.47 a.m. to say he had passed away. A few minutes after getting the call our bedroom turned from very dark to brilliant white. My husband couldn't see it; only I could. I felt it was my brother come to say goodbye because we couldn't get to the hospital.

Sheila and Peter, Alicante, Spain
Not too many people care to talk about this subject. I've always found it maybe a little frightening, but with those who you loved not so, which leads me to one experience. We had just returned from visiting our daughter. I take medication each morning but had not taken enough for the last three days so I wondered if I could do without the pill. After a few days I awoke in the early hours to a very strong smell of lavender. It was my dear grandmother's favourite lavender cologne. I

know she was telling me to continue taking my medication.

My most recent mystery involves a small mobile that we have. The mobile's origin is from Germany, and it consists of four animals one above the other – a horse, dog, cat and chicken. I noticed that one of the four mobiles was missing. I looked for it but found nothing. I told my husband and he also looked, with no luck. I then went to a cupboard to get my sewing machine. When I lifted the sewing machine there was the mobile. Despite my husband reattaching the piece tightly, it vanished again.

One of my most chilling experiences happened about thirty years ago in my sister's husband's house in Oregon, USA. My sister Pamela worked for a man named George and his wife for many years in their toy shop. They were German. Pam and her husband Fred loved George's house so when George died Pam and Fred bought the house. Strange and often dangerous things occurred in the house while they were living there; like saucepans being moved in front of the stove when grandchildren visited. Pam would often go into the kitchen and the cupboard doors would be all ajar, even though she had closed them. Once I went to stay with them. I lay in my en suite bath with my eyes closed. When I got out of the bath to find my clothes they had been moved, along with a soap holder, which had been hanging on the wall on a strong wooden ring. Pam later informed me that George had died in that bathroom. That night my bedroom door opened just enough for someone to look in.

None of this was imagined. I guess that's why we don't talk about it too much.

William, New Jersey, USA
I have had two experiences in the past and also now in the house I live in now. Generally I am not afraid of ghosts. I find it fascinating and I love to go to old buildings to admire the architecture and in the hope of having experiences.

My first experience was when I was renting a house in an extremely tiny town called Godeffroy, New York, USA. After living there for about a month, things started happening. There was about an inch high gap under the bathroom door, and the light could be seen coming from the other room. One night I was just stepping out of the shower and I saw someone's shadow walking past the door. My heart started racing as I thought for sure someone was in the house. I carefully opened the door and searched the house to find no one was there. I know it was a person's shadow without a doubt. This has happened on more than one occasion.

It has always been my nightly ritual to read in bed before going to sleep, and this would often be the time that strange happenings would occur. I always lock the doors when I went to bed. As I lay there reading, I would hear the back door open and close. I would get up to investigate, again thinking someone broke into the house, and the door would be closed and locked. This has happened many times to the point that I stopped investigating and just yelled at 'the ghost' to knock it off.

I used to collect water globes with music boxes built in and I had them on display in the living room. I would never allow anyone to touch them for fear of them getting broken and the only time I touched them was to dust them. They never got wound up. Oddly enough, there was one that was from the Broadway show the *Phantom of the Opera*. It had a black horse standing on its hind legs and the base had the Phantom's mask and other decor from the show and it played the song 'Music of the Night'.

This water globe, even though it wasn't wound up at all, would start to play just for two or three seconds every single night just after 11 p.m. like clockwork, to the point that I started having friends come over to see it for themselves. Unfortunately some of them stopped coming over my house after witnessing that. They stayed friends with me, but would not come in the house anymore.

While all of this was happening, I was having the same dream on many nights where there was an older guy with his left leg missing just below the knee. He was sitting on my couch arguing with me that it was his house not mine. That would be the extent of the dream, but this happened many nights.

One day I had a problem with the plumbing so I called my landlord and he came over with his wife. She and I sat in the kitchen talking while he worked on the drain and I asked them if they ever noticed strange things happening in the house. They said no, but my landlord's wife asked if I did. I was going to say no until she mentioned that she believes in ghosts. My landlord, on the other hand, did not. I told them what had been happening and when I mentioned the dream that I kept having, the expression on their faces went from interested and amused to very nervous and I knew something was not good.

I asked them what was wrong and they proceeded to tell me that before I rented the house, it belonged to my landlord's father, who recently passed away and who had lost his left leg below the knee due to diabetes, the same as the man in my dream. My landlord's wife ran home since they didn't live far from me and brought back a picture of her husband's father.

It was the man that I had argued with in my dream.

A couple of weeks after that, my landlord asked me if we could break the lease because it was bothering him to think that his father was upset that someone else was living in his house. I could understand his feelings, so as soon as I found another place to live I moved out.

The second experience I had was when I was living in Middletown, New Jersey, USA. I lived about fifteen minutes away from the Twin Lights Lighthouse in the Highlands. I love going to old buildings, so one day I decided to take a ride and visit the lighthouse. It sits way up on a hill. I drove all the way up the driveway and pulled into the parking lot, parked the car, and as I was walking towards the building, all of a sudden, this horrible fear came over me. I have never, ever felt fear like this before. I didn't see or hear anything, and I wasn't touched by anything, but for some reason I just had to get out of there. I literally ran back to my car and sped down that driveway. I have never been back since.

I want to go back and try again, but I will not go by myself. Every time I tell someone about it and ask them to go with me, they just laugh. I don't know if it's because they don't believe me and think I'm being ridiculous, or they're afraid of what they will feel if they go – maybe a little of both. I will be back one day.

My most recent experience is happening now. I live in Manahawkin, New Jersey, USA, just off of Long Beach Island. My life partner of twenty-four years passed away a year ago in May. Since then, there are times where I feel like he is in the room with me. It's hard to explain, but it's as if you're sitting in a chair and your loved one comes in the room behind you. You don't have to see him or her, but you know they're there. It's that kind of feeling.

Just last night I was sitting watching television and my dog was curled up sleeping, then all of a sudden he quickly raised his head and kept staring at one spot. I tried to get his attention, asking what was wrong, but he wouldn't even look my way. He just kept staring, so I went over to where he was and I was kneeling in front of him talking to him and he kept looking around as if he was trying to see something.

All of a sudden I heard paper rustling behind me. I turned around and the paper that I had sitting on the coffee table was lying on the floor. I know it didn't fall off, because it was sitting towards the middle of the coffee table and the windows were all closed so there was no wind to blow it off. I just said hello to him, told him I loved and missed him, but to stop making a mess.

When he was alive, he had a bad habit of leaving the upper kitchen cabinet doors open and I have banged my head on them on more than one occasion. Recently on two occasions so far, I have walked into the kitchen and some of the upper cabinet doors would be open – not completely, like he used to do, but just enough for me to notice. I like to think it's his way to let me know he's still here with me. I know it isn't the doors malfunctioning because the magnets that hold them closed are so strong that you have to tug on them to open them.

Angie, Ireland
My name is Angela and I'm seventeen years old. My dad died on 11 December, 2002 and it was a few days later when this incident occurred.

I was extremely upset and decided to sleep in my mam's bed for the night. I remember feeling quite restless and unable to sleep when I turned onto my side. I was facing the bedroom door, which leads out onto the landing, when I saw an image. It looked exactly like smoke from a fire except it was on the landing. It was white and did not appear to be moving. I suddenly felt calmer and knew in my own heart and soul that it was my dad giving me a sign.

In all my years, I know I'll never forget that night.

Pat, County Westmeath, Ireland
In 2005 I was working on a woodwork project in Mullingar Industrial Estate.

It was the 9 November at 11.55 a.m., just before lunchtime. The project was coming on fine. I was the last one in the workshop at the time.

I turned around and to my amazement a young man about twenty years old was sitting on a box taking interest in what I was doing.

I looked at him and he looked at me, then he just vanished into thin air. As he was only less than a metre away I got to see in detail what he was wearing. His legs were not entirely visible, only from his knee to hip; he was wearing black trousers but his legs merged into the box.

He was a pleasant sort of lad but said nothing. I went to another room to tell a colleague. As I explained what I had just seen I noticed my two arms were covered in large goose pimples. I'm not a religious person so I eventually came up with my own logical explanation.

Shirley and Lou, West Indies

It's difficult to know where to start because I have many, many stories of the kind you are looking for, spread over the seven Caribbean islands on which my family and I lived.

The Lady Behind The Bed

My husband and I own and manage a guesthouse on Montserrat; the island is often called 'The Other Emerald Isle' because of the island's close historical ties with Ireland and the similarity in its geology, landscapes, and the speech and personality of its nationals. Because of my own Irish heritage, our guest-house is called 'Erindell'.

Most children love an ice-cold glass of lemonade or limeade, especially on a hot day. The day on which I found the hidden bottle of 'lemonade' was definitely a hot day. I was dawdling here and there around the apartment, bored, opening drawers and cupboards and examining their contents. To my surprise, when I opened the cupboard under the kitchen sink, I found a bottle full of 'lemonade'.

Or so I thought.

Not stopping to think why a bottle of lemonade would be under the kitchen sink, I opened the cap, put the bottle to my lips and drank heartily. Then I realised that something was terribly wrong. Suddenly it didn't taste like lemonade at all. In fact it was kerosene! My stomach heaved and I remember vomiting, then nothing more until I woke up in bed, weak and drained, but alive.

Then a feeling came over me that I was not alone in the room. I looked up and saw a lady standing behind the bedstead, her hands holding onto the metal rail above my pillow. She was dressed in long flowing robes of white, and there was a pale blue veil on her head. She looked down at me and smiled, but said nothing. I smiled back at her, and from that moment I felt peaceful and happy and sure that I would get well.

Later, when Mammy came in to check on me, I told her about the lady behind the bed and asked her who it was. Mammy laughed and said there was no one there and that I must have been dreaming. Besides, the bedstead was pushed up against the partition so it was impossible for anyone to stand there. As Mammy left the room, she turned her head towards me and in a quiet voice said, 'It must have been your guardian angel!' Actually, from the description and colour of her robes and veil, I believe it was Blessed Mary, the mother of Jesus and protector of children who had stood guard over my bed!

Strange Happenings at Daddy's Funeral

My father, retired Attorney General of Montserrat, had been languishing for some time, his lungs riddled with cancer from years of smoking. I had finished work at the medical college where I was administrative assistant to the president as well as human resource manager. It had been a tiring week, so on my way home that Friday afternoon I took a pit stop at the Evergreen Tree in Plymouth, the capital, and wearily sat on the wall licking an ice cream cone.

Montserratians swear that if one waited long enough at the Evergreen Tree, one could see everybody who lived on the island, and no wonder, as it was the centre of town. It was minutes to five o'clock when Dr Ronnie Cooper passed by in his car and called out to me, 'Shirley, what are you doing there? Your father is dead!'

I said, 'What! When did that happen?'

'This afternoon!' he shouted. 'They've already taken him to the morgue. Your mother tried, but couldn't reach you at the college.'

A tooting car horn behind him made Dr Cooper drive on, and I sat on the wall stunned, ice cream dripping all over my hand.

My father, Basil Fitzpatrick Dias, MBE (Member of the British Empire), was the son of a Portuguese landowner from Madeira who had settled in St Kitts and had acquired a sugar estate in Sandy Point. Happily ensconced at Lambert's Estate, Grandfather Andrew Dias practiced smuggling as a pastime in addition to other legitimate business.

He fathered many children by different village women. Some of these offspring we only knew after he'd adopted them all and given them the Dias name. Not surprisingly, the St Kitts telephone directory has numerous Dias's listed.

To appease his conscience, I suppose, Grandfather Dias remained a good Roman Catholic to his dying day. He made sure he paid his dues to the Church and sent his son off to a seminary to become a priest. That situation didn't last long however. My father – tall, dark and handsome – came home to St Kitts from the seminary on his first summer holidays and met my mother, the vivacious and musically talented Edith Brookes. But that's another story!

Although not destined to be a priest, Daddy's deep faith in the Roman Catholic Church held him in good stead throughout his life, and no living person dared to interfere with any of us. But the dead follow no such rules. Daddy's funeral was a large one, as he was well known and highly respected throughout the Caribbean. Attending the funeral were judges and lawyers he had worked with throughout his long legal career, civil servants and hundreds of other people, some of them ex-convicts he had 'put away' while in office.

The day of the funeral was rainy with gray clouds hanging heavily in the sky. Mammy, my sister Linda, my brother David and I were in the last car to leave the Dias family home on Richmond Hill, overlooking Plymouth, the capital. Mammy requested that I drive.

As I backed out of the carport, Mammy suddenly told me to stop the car, and she asked David to go back and make sure all the doors were locked. David 'stoopsed' (made a rude sound) and looked pissed, but obeyed. He went back and checked both the front door and garage door. They were locked. The funeral itself was with pomp and circumstance. There were Daddy's favourite hymns, usual platitudes and pouring rain.

After the last graveside hymn was sung, we left the cemetery and headed home where, at least, it would be dry and where the dining table was heaped with food supplied by friends and neighbours. Our car was the first one to arrive back at the house.

No amount of words can describe our shock when we entered the driveway and found the front door wide open. We had all seen Mammy lock the doors on leaving the house, and had watched David go back and check the doors. No one else had a key except Mammy. To add to the disturbing scene, there was a large black dog stretched out across the open doorway, its head resting on its paws.

We were still standing by the car, not knowing quite what to do, when other cars started to drive up and park. Everyone there saw the dog.

'Whose dog is it?'

'I don't know.'

'Could it be one of the Edwards's dogs?'

'No, that's not one of theirs!'

'It's not one of ours,' Eileen Edwards confirmed.

'It doesn't have on a collar!'

'I wonder who it belongs to?'

The questions went on and on but no one, including the Richmond Hill residents, could identify the black dog.

'Shoo!' someone shouted at last. The dog didn't budge, not even a muscle. We ended up having to step over the animal to get inside the house. When we were all inside, not talking too much, the dog got up and entered the house behind us, walking over to stand in front of Daddy's favourite armchair.

You could have heard a pin drop. After a while, people began filling plates with food, so no one saw when the dog left. It was there one minute and gone the next.

A little later, when everybody was wandering about with their plates, Mammy asked me to make sure that Father Bulla had been given something to eat. He had been one of the officiating priests at the funeral and a close family friend. I looked around but couldn't find him. Perhaps he'd gone to the bathroom I thought, as I crossed the drawing room heading towards the bedroom. That's when I saw him.

Father Bulla was in my parents' bedroom wearing his vestments. He held an open prayer book in one hand and a small vial of holy water in the other. As he prayed, he sprinkled holy water all over the room, and then he repeated this in the other two bedrooms. I retreated quickly and never told Mammy what I'd seen.

Next morning, Mammy phoned me at home and asked if I'd been back to their house that night. I said 'no, why?' She said I should come over and see something. What she showed me was very strange indeed. On the ground in front of every doorway, someone had poured a line of table salt. There was also salt around Mammy's car in the carport and on the car itself!

I know that salt is supposed to be a deterrent against evil. But who could have put it there? Obviously it had been one of the persons who had witnessed the black dog and wanted to do something to help the family. That person must have returned to the house during the night and poured the salt!

Father Bulla passed away a few years later, and so did Mammy who was convinced that the black dog was Daddy's spirit that had come back to check up on her. In fact, she told me that she sensed Daddy's spirit in the house many times, and that it gave her a feeling of peace.

She also said that she knew the exact moment when he came to say goodbye to her, finally convinced that she would be taken care of by all their children.

What I didn't know, until Linda told me recently, was that the black dog had left paw prints where it stood in front of Daddy's armchair. She told me the paw prints were not left in dust, but had actually sunk into the dark red ceramic tiles where they can still be seen today!

Unfortunately the house lies in the exclusion zone covered with volcanic ash, so there is little chance I can go back there and see for myself. The salt donor has never come forward, so I guess we'll never be able to solve the mystery of Daddy's funeral!

Steve, Chesire, UK

Four years ago, unexpectedly, I developed a really serious heart condition and, having been admitted to hospital, I fell into a coma for two weeks. It was apparent that I had 'broken' the mitral valve in my heart. During this time my family were called into the hospital several times to say goodbye as the doctors believed I wasn't going to survive.

However, I woke up in a different hospital having had a new mechanical mitral valve replacement, and a triple bypass was carried out for good measure.

I cannot describe how weak I felt after this operation and it took several weeks before I could manage to ease myself out of bed and into the chair next to my bed. The first time I managed this on my own I was feeling quite pleased with myself for the achievement and enjoying the fact that I could sit up. The ward I was in was only made up of four beds and my chair was in one of the corners. As I looked over to the opposite corner I could see a transparent cloud swirling around just below ceiling height. I could best describe this as looking at the same type of medium as portrayed in the film *Predator*, though this had no shape. The cloud appeared to be gathering in a faster and faster vortex.

I was fascinated by this and strangely didn't feel threatened at all. I did get the feeling at the time that this was meant for me and sure enough it made a direct line for me and hit me on the top of my head. I threw my head back in the chair and I remember thinking *just go with it.*

It felt like I was being filled up with something and could feel the sensation coming up my legs and body until it reached my head. Immediately after it was over I felt as though I had been sprayed with something fizzy like lucozade. I did feel that I had been energized somewhat. I remember this event absolutely clearly and I do not believe that I was hallucinating. I mention that experience as it was the first of a number I subsequently had.

The most outstanding of these for me was my experience of my late father. Whilst in hospital I had an overwhelming desire to visit my mum and dad's grave. I promised myself that when I was discharged from hospital I would make it one of my first visits.

My daughter picked me up one morning and we went to the cemetery. I went to my parents' grave and paid my respects; I told them how grateful I was that I had been given another chance at this life.

I then said to my daughter that I would like to go to my sister's grave, which is in another part of the cemetery. We walked down the path a few yards when I heard my dad cough from behind me. Oddly I had no desire to turn around and look at him. It was as though I just accepted the fact that he was there and simultaneously I was certain I could smell his presence. I said to my daughter, 'Dad's here with me.'

Just at that point I felt extremely tired and felt like I couldn't take another step. I said that I needed to sit down and sat on a low drystone wall that ran down the edge of the path. Out of the corner of my left eye I saw my dad sit down next to me, easing up his trouser legs as he did so. I turned to him and sadly he was gone.

Immediately I felt my energy return and I was able to resume walking. One of the surprising things for me about this is the smell. I could not describe it to anyone, not even myself – before or after – but at the time I knew immediately it was my dad's own personal smell. It came across very strong, not just a whiff as perhaps you might expect.

I wanted to share my experience in the hope that similar pieces of evidence of the continuation of the soul are found in other people's experiences.

Stephen, Canada
The following is a very personal experience that has profoundly affected my life. It is sacred to me.

In the summer of 1980, I was bicycling in the Maritime provinces of Canada, painting and travelling on the funding of the Canada Council, a short-term grant of three months duration. Funny enough, I had applied for a larger grant to do this project in Ireland for a year's duration. As I was still a young artist at the time, the Council granted me funding for this shorter duration.

During one of my stopovers at a place called Shediac, New Brunswick, I had set up camp along the seashore of the Northumberland Strait. It was a fantastic bright sunny day and one to inspire me to paint the seascape that laid itself out for me. The beach was deserted and the town itself was about ten miles (a little over fifteen kilometres) to the west of where I had set up my small canvas tent.

The ocean breeze was refreshing and I set up my drawing board upon my lap to commence painting. My bare feet were immersed in the surf and I was not aware of the sun burning on my ankles. The sea was quite cold and I was totally engrossed in executing the painting before me.

Within three hours, as I nearly completed the painting, I noticed that my ankles were now severely burned. I hadn't felt the burn but the open blisters and weeping wounds alarmed me that I had suffered very severe sunburn. My ankles were swollen to three times their normal size. Walking was extremely painful and cycling was out of the question.

I had the presence of mind to apply a mechanic's soap, which I carried to replace the lubricant in my ball bearings of my bike as well as to take off the grease whenever I had to change bike parts, to the open wounds. Fortunately for me this wasn't a greasy substance and would serve me well as not to take any more skin when I finally did get to the hospital.

But at that moment, I wasn't sure I'd get to a hospital or any other place where people would be. To make matters worse, the sun was now fading on the horizon and I started to shake uncontrollably due to the loss of body heat escaping for my ankles. I realised I would be on my own for the night with a fever coming on and no way to contact anyone.

I didn't have the energy to gather firewood or light a fire. The wind had just picked up and I moved to better anchor my tent support lines in the sand by tying the guide ropes to large rocks and burying those into the sand deeper than the stakes had been.

In my wrecked condition, I crawled into my tent and secured my food, water and art supplies as best I could. The howling of the wind and shaking of the tent told me I would be in for the ride of my life. The night air grew colder as the sand does not hold heat after the sun sets.

I unrolled my sleeping bag. As my tent had a small leak in it, the plastic I would have used to cover my bike now served as a large sleeve for the sleeping bag to keep the water off me.

I tried to get some sleep as a relief from the burning pain of my ankles. Try as I might I could not keep warm. I curled up into a fetal position to conserve my body heat. The balm of lubricant soap was stopping the drain of fluid from my ankles. I was praying that I would survive the night. I'd worry about decamping in the morning and getting back to civilisation then.

As I laid there wrecked and shaking from the cold and fever, I closed my eyes trying to bring on sleep. I couldn't relax enough to allow sleep to come. In the darkness of my closed eyes, I saw a spirit come to my tent. I opened my eyes, fully conscious but unable to see a thing. I closed my eyes again and this personage then was entering my tent.

Again I opened my eyes to see only the emptiness of the tent and hear sounds of the wind howling and tent flapping vigorously. Again, I closed my eyes to observe the spirit who was of immense height. I would guess he stood over seven feet tall, but this didn't make any sense as my tent was barely three feet by five feet and no higher than four feet and I could never stand up fully within this shell.

The spirit could only be seen with my eyes fully closed. I knew I was in trouble medically and I now thought I was becoming delusional. How could I trust me senses? What did strike me at this very moment was the range of phenomena that occurred simultaneously.

First, allow me to describe this extra dimensional being. I felt a profound peace overcome me as I looked upon this gentle giant. He appeared as one would expect to see from the Old Testament. His hair was long and white. His face showed age but immense intelligence. His beard was as white as his hair. He wore an animal skin coat that was dyed in a range of colours in horizontal bands.

These colours appeared to have been made from natural agents, perhaps berries, stains, or earthen mixtures. He had a presence that radiated that he had a life of many long years, beyond the ones he had lived on earth. His form was very much human, superhuman even. I had never felt such calmness as I felt at that moment.

Next, the air in the tent was completely still. Even as the wind slammed against the outside of the tent shell, all was still inside the thin plastic walls of the tent. I couldn't raise myself because I was too weak. But I felt no need to raise myself. The benevolence of this person calmed me in a way that no words were ever spoken or even needed to explain that he was there for my safety and comfort. I had never trusted anything or anyone in this way before.

I just knew I would be saved. To my amazement, time had seemed to stand still and what would seem to have transpired in fifteen minutes or so, was but a very brief few seconds. My body had ceased its shaking. I could relax completely and started to uncurl my body to fill the length of the sleeping bag.

What was the most remarkable part of this experience was how I felt the hands of this sage starting to fold and tuck the plastic that surrounded my sleeping bag around me in such a manner that it became an incubator. As I drew breath from outside the plastic, I exhaled directly into the folded plastic bag, inflating it with the warm air of my breath.

I did not have the presence of mind to perform these life-saving mechanics. I didn't have the strength to do it even if I had thought of it. I was in a state of complete euphoria. As quickly as this realisation overtook me, so did sleep. I didn't witness his departure. I was out in a flash, warmed by this experience as much as by the incubator that miraculously saved my life that night.

I awoke the next morning recalling what I had just experienced. I was re-energized enough to break camp and cycle to the next largest city of Moncton where I boarded a train that morning to get to a hospital in Saint John, New Brunswick (my place of birth even though I now reside in Ontario).

I have tried to place who this being was. He was not a relative that I was aware of. He did not fit any of the descriptions of the Old Testament, the New Testament, the Book of Mormon or the Doctrines and Covenants.

To this day I do not know who saved my life, other that a spiritual being. I recall nothing was asked of me at that moment and it didn't seem important to him that I know who my benefactor was.

I have kept this experience close for these many years, sharing it only with close family and trusted friends.

My name is Stephen John. I am college educated and have exhibited my paintings internationally, having resided in France for two years in the nineties. I am comforted that there is 'something' beyond this reality and beings departed or otherwise for us yet to reside with.

Anon., County Westmeath, Ireland
While on my way into the graveyard one day to visit my husband's grave I noticed a man tidying up a grave where there was a recent plot. When I left my husband's grave the man I saw had vanished. I mentioned this to other people I happened to meet and they saw nothing. However, I got a very eerie feeling and made my departure as fast as I could.

A very good friend of mine has been dead for years. She had been a very regular visitor to my house and we usually sat out in the garden. As I was sitting out in my garden on a very sunny day I experienced a strange feeling of her presence. However, on opening my front door a neighbour a few doors down approached to tell me that my friend's daughter was seriously ill in hospital. I went to see her and am happy to saw she made a full recovery.

Lee, Scotland

My Grandparent's old farm house at Easter Bendochy Farm near Coupar Angus in Perthshire, Scotland, was a magic place. Not only was it in the middle of nowhere and full of places for us kids to explore, it's also where I had my first real encounter with a ghost!

The house was a huge imposing white building and was built in the middle of a Celtic cross (which is evident from ariel photographs), and is one of the reasons I felt it oozed energy.

Ghost stories were rife, as with all places of a certain age, and my grandad used to thrill us with tales of ghostly footsteps on the gravel outside the house at night and of ghostly sightings throughout the house and its outbuildings. One of the most curious things about the farm was the constant feeling of being watched, particularly when you past the old 'tattie shed' where the potatoes were stored.

My younger brother, Stuart, and I were always keen to explore these same buildings as kids and this particularly warm weekend in the mid 1980s was no different. Two young guys asked Grandad if they could store their stock car in one of the outbuildings while they worked on it, and he agreed that they could. Stuart and I were more than keen to see what the guys were doing and watched silently through the open door as they hammered and drilled for what seemed like hours.

We were in the old barn, where the combine harvester was kept, and at the back of the barn there was an access door to the old grain loft that hadn't been used for years. The door was open and the sunlight was streaming through.

As we watched the guys at work on their car I suddenly became aware I was being watched. It was a very creepy feeling and I remember turning around to look up at the grain loft door. Just then, I saw the figure of a man silhouetted by the sun standing in the doorway.

I stared up at him but he didn't move and as I turned back to Stuart a freezing wind blew right past me, and it was strong enough to blow my hair back. I looked back at the grain loft and the figure was gone. I was freaked out and took off – hotly pursued by a bemused Stuart – back to the house to relay the story to my grandparents.

Later that night, when I brought up the ghostly encounter again, grandad told me: 'Dinnae worry about that, lassie, it would just be Auld Jock.'

It turned out that 'Auld Jock' was a farm employee back at the turn of the twentieth century who, after being caught allegedly embezzling from the estate, took a shotgun and killed himself – in the tattie shed. Seems I wasn't the only one to have seen him, either, as grandad also knew of and had felt his presence.

The next day there was a knock at the door – it was one of the guys who had been working on his stock car. Gran came through and asked Stuart and I if we had taken a crash helmet as the guys were missing it. We had, of course, no idea what they were talking about. To this day, the crash helmet never reappeared – and I can say, hand on heart, we never touched it.

A few years later, just a few weeks before my grandparents were due to leave the farm, when grandad retired, I wandered down the old road for a walk with

Gran and their collie dog, Tess. Tess was daft on playing with tennis balls and you would always find one lying at your feet during a walk. I remember throwing it for her and it flew into the tattie shed; she went in after it with great gusto but ten or fifteen minutes later she emerged without it.

Now, anyone who has ever had any dealings with Border Collies will know they're nothing if not dogmatic. She had never before failed to come back with a ball – but this one was, it seemed, gone. I went in after Tess but no sign of the bright red and yellow ball, even though the shed was nigh near empty. Another mystery: was it Jock at work?

The day finally came for them to leave the farm and my grandad, my mum, Catherine, and I were the last to leave the old place before it was torn down. As I climbed into the back of the car ready to head to their new place, I paused for a second and looked over at the tattie shed and whispered: 'Bye Jock, look after yourself.' I swear to this day the energy at the place that day was almost tangible.

Many years later I visited a spirit medium for a reading. Midway through, after very welcome messages from my Great Gran Kate, the woman paused and said she had a question for me.

She asked: 'Lee, does the name Jock mean anything to you?' I smiled and half laughed as I said: 'Jock from Bendochy?' Just then the flame on the candle next to me grew substantially in size quite suddenly, and I drew back. However, the woman just smiled and said: 'It's ok, it is Jock and he is just letting you know he's pleased you remembered him. He says he was a simple man and would never have hurt you.' I smiled and said to thank him for coming through. It was so good to know all of those magic times had not been in my head!

Now the old farm has been turned into several luxury homes, including one right on the site of the old tattie shed. I often drive past and wonder how many things the people in that house have 'lost' or how many shadows they cannot explain. One thing's for sure, it's probably just 'Auld Jock from Bendochy' having a laugh!

John, Ireland

My wife, Lily, passed away on 15 February 1980.
About two weeks after the funeral, I was lying in my bed wide awake, unable to sleep this particular night. It was three o'clock in the morning because I remember looking at the clock. Suddenly I felt the bed sheets over me being pulled by unseen hands towards the end of the bed. I got pretty scared I can tell you! I started to pull them back up, but each time they were being pulled away from me. I started to ask questions saying, 'Lily, is that you?' But, of course, I got no reply. After about two to three minutes, it suddenly stopped.

The following Monday night, I mentioned it to friends of mine at a prayer group I was in at that time. They all agreed that it was my late wife trying to tell me that I wasn't to worry about her anymore, that she was at peace, and had moved on to the other side.

So I felt good about that, and it helped me to move on a bit with my life.

Peter, County Longford, Ireland

Back in the summer of 1967 I had left my girlfriend home and was walking up the Battery Road (in Longford) home. It was about 11.30 p.m. on a Tuesday night. I suddenly froze; it felt like I had been dipped in a block of ice. I felt every hair on my head being pulled up. I am not easily scared, I nonetheless did not have the courage to take my hands out of my pockets. In a matter of seconds the feeling disappeared and I continued home. It bothered me so much that I told a friend.

The following Friday night, after we had both left our girlfriends home and were passing the same spot, I asked my mate to wait on the path and in order to face this fear I climbed the wall of the graveyard. I proceeded to stumble down the graveyard, tripping over briars, headstones, sunken graves, etc. – and upon returning to the footpath we continued home. The experience has never bothered me since but has remained vividly in my memory.

On another note, whilst in Adelaide, South Australia, I awoke in the early hours of the morning, with the conviction that my father had died back home in Longford. My crying awoke my then wife. She comforted me and we went back to sleep. A few weeks later I learned that my grandfather on my mother's side had died around about the time I had awoken.

Again in Australia, one Friday morning I awoke with a heavy weight on my chest. When I went to work I was asked by my mate Maurice why I was so quiet. I replied, 'That bloody daughter of mine is in trouble.' That was what I had felt.

The same afternoon Maurice's wife asked why I was troubled. I told her, 'I think my mother is sick.' That evening I found out my mother had died.

Before my mother's death, and a week before my birthday, I had this heavy melancholy feeling. On my birthday I was so down that I didn't want to celebrate. I went to a strange pub south of the city of Adelaide where nobody would know me. About 8 p.m. a friend, Vincent, came in looking for me. He came up to me and before he spoke I said, 'My father is dead.'

He replied, 'Oh, has Pat [my ex-wife] got in touch with you?'

I said 'No, I just know.' The family had rang my ex-wife earlier. We went to our local in the north east of Adelaide, about twelve miles from where Vincent had caught up with me.

5

Music

Music can create a strong and unbreakable bond between friends and family members. A special song or piece of music can hold huge significance in people's relationships. The contributors to this chapter have experienced such pieces of music cropping up in their lives after the death of a loved one. These experiences are seen as comforting signs from their lost friend or family member that they are still with them.

Brenda, Location Unknown
My mother, Phyliss Rowe, (nee Cunningham) passed away in February 2010 at the age of eighty-three. She grew up on a subsistence farm and had been a subservient housewife. Her life was one of drudgery and compliance. She'd shared her hopes and dreams about how she'd have liked her life to be if she'd been free to make her choices and told me she'd always wanted to be a pianist.

She shared with me her belief that this world can provide everything a person needs to live, and if it wasn't for men getting into fights and starting wars everybody would just be having fun because that's what life is meant for.

I don't remember ever seeing her have any fun, though occasionally herself and my dad would get dressed up and go out on a date to listen to a honkey tonk piano player.

A few months after she died, my son, her grandson, told me he'd seen her in a dream. He said he saw her playing honky tonk music on a grand piano and she was having so much fun. I didn't talk to my son about what my mom and I shared, and she didn't have any opportunities to share her hopes and dreams with him.

He couldn't have known that playing the piano and having fun was the life she wanted to live. I think she's alive on the other side and her hopes and dreams for herself have come true.

My faith in there being more to life than just the years from birth to death is stronger then ever now.

David, Manchester, UK

I was born in 1949 and as a very young child, certainly under four years of age, I was apparently fascinated by a song that was out around that time called 'Buttons and Bows'. Naturally I was too young to remember and I don't have any memories of it other than what my mother told me.

In the early sixties, probably 1962 or 1963 there was an upbeat version made of this song, I think by Tommy Bruce, which was very popular for a few weeks.

Every time it was played on the radio or TV, my mother reiterated how I used to go daft whenever I heard the song, laughing and bouncing about while it played. Obviously it brought back fond memories for my mother of when I was a very young child and I always associated the song with me and my mother.

On the afternoon of 10 December 1985 my mother died in hospital. I was the only one at her bedside and she just simply went to sleep. The following day something went wrong with the exhaust on my car. I can't remember exactly what it was but it was serious and I had to get it repaired straightaway. I drove it to a tyre and exhaust specialist in Cheetham Hill about six or seven miles from where I lived in Manchester.

Normally they fix it while you wait but the part was out of stock and they had to send to another branch. They told me it would be about two hours so I went for a walk to the shopping precinct. Walking through the precinct there was a busker playing 'Buttons and Bows'.

Maybe a bizarre coincidence, but it is almost fifty years now since that song left the charts in the early sixties and in all that time I have never heard it mentioned let alone played except on that afternoon twenty-five years ago about twenty-four hours after my mother died.

William James Peter, Ontario, Canada
Our ancestors emigrated to Newfoundland from Ireland during the potato famines between the 1830s and 1850s.

My father, the youngest of ten, was a devout Catholic but more importantly he was a good Christian man. He had his final stroke on New Year's Eve 1998. The family met with Dad's doctor who advised us to let him go, but he lived on for another nine to ten days, still saying his rosary while in a coma. The priest attending Dad finally said, 'We should be praying to him not for him.'

My younger brother and sister remembered an occasion while with Dad they heard Sara Brightman singing 'Time to say Goodbye' so they arranged to play it during the vigil the night before the funeral and again at the graveside. The song stuck firmly in my mind as my wife and I flew back to Toronto.

In Toronto I used the subway to travel to and from work. The Toronto subway system allows buskers to play in its stations. I was not back home a week when a group was playing 'Time to say Goodbye' as I was changing trains one morning. This went on about once a week for about three months.

My wife dropped me at another subway station one morning as she had a meeting downtown. I'll be damned as I went into this different station the group was now there playing 'Time to say Goodbye'. I went up to the group leader and told him the story and he became quite spooked too.

Later that summer, now nine months after my father's death I was watching a Sara Brightman special on TV. My wife had gone to bed so I had the sound turned up and was having a good sob as Sara sang 'Time to say Goodbye'. Suddenly the photo of my father and stepmother which sat atop the TV cabinet flew off and fell to the floor. Oddly enough it did not break!

I regret that I did not inherit my father's great faith; I rarely go to church, only for funerals mostly. Yet when my kids are having some problem I have them pray to my father. It never fails they say!

Fionnula, County Longford, Ireland

After my dear mum, Alice, died I was reminded of her, particularly when I was holidaying abroad.

My mother often mentioned in passing that she would love to see Lourdes and she was a devoted Catholic. For her birthday in June of 1990 a few years before she died, I booked tickets for us both to Lourdes.

She was in awe of the Grotto, especially during the torchlight procession in the evenings.

I returned some years later and stayed in the same hotel. One night there was a sing song in the bar and the first song that was sung was 'Living Next Door to Alice'.

I knew in my heart that my mother was with me on my journey in a spiritual way. Amen.

6

Aroma

In this chapter the contributors felt the presence of their loved ones through the medium of smell, oftentimes through the familiar scent of perfume, the aroma of their favourite flowers or their cigarette smoke.

M., Alicante, Spain

My mother and I were very close and saw each other every day until she died in 1995, aged ninety-five. We used to discuss how she would let me know she was close to me after her death. She herself decided on the smell of flowers, especially carnations, because they were her wedding flowers in 1927.

To this day when I have had bad news or problems in the family my sitting room always smells of carnations, as if she is there to let me know she is sharing it with me. I lived in England for sixty years before coming to live in Spain eight years ago and I can still smell carnations when there are no flowers in the room.

My mother was Irish and I do believe she wanted to continue her contact with the family she left behind.

Jean, Manchester, UK

Over the years I am certain that my mum and dad are sometimes very close to me. Firstly my dad died forty-two years ago and the night he passed away I was alone at home. Obviously I was very upset and couldn't sleep.

After a time I heard someone call my name. I got up to see if there was anyone at the door, then went back to bed. It was then that I felt someone pat my shoulder a couple of times. It was a comforting feeling and there was a sense of peace in the room.

The next day my mum told me what had happened to her – it was exactly the same time and the same experience that I had had. I am positive it was my dad visiting us as we were very close.

I can still often smell the perfume of my mum and the cigarette smoke of my dad in my house. I always say 'Hello, have you come to me?'

You can sense that there is someone around.

Now people may say that every one can smell something and it's just your imagination but the fact is I have had no sense of smell for the past fifteen years and indeed often burn my cooking because of this!

I firmly believe that our loved ones are near us.

Susan, Wales

My father was born in October 1908 and died of a heart attack on 29 January 1970, two weeks before I was due to marry. Prior to his death, he was the manager of the largest Liverpool Victoria office in England, where we had moved to from Wales. Dad was always im-maculately dressed for work and kept his hair 'short back and sides'. When it started to grow over the tops of his ears but he didn't really need a haircut, he would stand in front of the kitchen mirror and use his lighter to singe away the stragglers! Being a Brylcreem user, on occasion, his hair would actually flare up as he put the flame to it! He would jump around cursing and bat the flame out with his hand. As he used to give me a lift to work each day, I was always in the kitchen to witness this spectacle and smell the awful stench of singeing hair. It really used to make me laugh though and I told him that one day his whole head would catch fire!

About four days after Dad's death, my husband (at that time my fiancé) was standing in our kitchen and as I walked in I could smell really strongly something burning. I asked him if he had put anything in the Ideal Boiler (which used coke) and he said he hadn't and couldn't smell anything.

I realised then that the smell was only in front of the mirror at head height and it was actually the smell of burning hair. My fiancé could smell it too when he stood in front of the mirror. I took it as a sign that my dad was happy and trying to make me laugh. Although it was upsetting, it comforted me greatly.

I got married on Valentines Day 1970, a bittersweet day for me. I have four older siblings and one younger but I was the only one that my dad did not see get married. We moved into a rented flat which my dad had organised for us.

About ten months after we moved in, I was walking past a mirror in our hall when I smelt my dad's hair singeing. I just said 'Hello Dad' and felt so pleased that he was able to be in my home.

In 1972 we bought our first home in Rayleigh, Essex. We had been in there about a year and, once again, as I walked past a mirror in the hall, the smell of singeing hair assailed me. Once again, I just spoke to my dad and thanked him for visiting our new home. It gave me a marvellous feeling of well-being.

We emigrated to New Zealand from Rayleigh in July 1974. For a month, we rented a flat and then moved into a two bedroom bungalow which we had purchased. I was working for just over a year when I found out I was pregnant. We decided we needed to decorate the spare bedroom in readiness for the new arrival and before we could do that, we had to sort out the few boxes which had never been opened since our initial move and were stacked in the room. My husband was at work one Saturday when I made a start on the project. The previous owner had left a mirror hanging from a picture rail in the room.

I picked up a box and as I stepped toward the wall where the mirror was – I smelled singeing hair! Not as strong as previously but, there was no doubt in my mind what the smell was. I thought it was incredible that my dad had followed me to New Zealand and I was delighted to think that he probably knew I was pregnant too.

We returned to the UK in 1978 and in four further houses I had exactly the same experience. Over the years, the smell has diminished greatly but it is such a distinctive smell that even the faintest whiff cannot be mistaken.

My mother was born in February 1910 and died January 2003, thirty-three years after my father. She missed him every day of her life. She always promised me that if there was any way she could get a message to us after she died she would. The night she died, I was sleeping alone as I was suffering with a badly frozen shoulder. I awoke with a start at 1.30 a.m. and wondered what had woken me.

As I lay there listening, I felt a hand rest on top of my head and I can only describe it as a 'tinkling' passing through my head down through my body and out of my feet. I knew in that instant that my mother had died and had come to say goodbye to me on her way. I was absolutely heartbroken and on two occasions in the first days after her death, I would feel the warmth of an arm being put around my back. Then, absolutely nothing more until 2007. I left work and went home for some lunch. As I was preparing my food, I just thought to myself *I wonder if mam and dad are together because that's all she ever wanted*. I didn't give it another thought, picked up my food and sat in the garden whilst I ate.

When I got into my car to return to work, I leant forward to put the key in the ignition and as I sat back, the smell of my dad's hair singeing in front of my rear-view mirror was so strong that I burst out crying! I know he was telling me that my mam had fulfilled her dying wish to be reunited with him. Before she died, she promised me that 'The day you die, I will be up early that morning to meet you!' I'm positive she will and probably my dad too.

How wonderful!

S., Manchester, UK

My husband passed away ten years ago this November 14th. Every New Year's Eve I believe that he is with me. I can smell his aftershave.

Sometimes he moves the Christmas cards and I can also feel him next to me in bed; not all the time, but sometimes. I also know he is in our house as I can feel him. I hope this doesn't seem silly because to me it is very very real.

Irene, Alicante, Spain

My late father and my son are often about, although their presence is often felt rather than seen. Dad smoked a particular type of cigarette with quite a distinctive smell.

My son died on Mother's Day and I often feel he is about. I have also sensed him quite close. I have a friend who actually sees both of them.

On a recent trip to the UK she came to see us and afterwards she said that my son was standing behind my car. She thought there was something wrong with the car. We had to get something minor done to it which was what he was trying to tell her. When she came on a second visit she told me he was sitting close by.

Many years ago, shortly after Dad passed away, I had reason to be out one evening. My husband wasn't very well and when I got home he told me that Dad had been keeping him company.

These things don't bother either of us, in fact they are quite comforting.

Kathleen, Cheshire, UK

My dear father, William Marchant, died on 7 December 1991 at almost ninety years of age. He suffered from emphysema and although he was really fed up near the end, he felt very sad about leaving loved ones behind.

Nineteen days after Daddy's death, on Boxing Day, I had my four sons and daughter plus grandchildren around to our house for a family get-together. During the afternoon, one of our sons came to me in the kitchen and said, 'There's a terrible smell in the lounge Mum, has the cat peed in the corner?' The smell lasted about four minutes and was a mixture of tomcat pee and burning wire. This smell disappeared as quickly as it came.

I didn't think anymore of it until a week later. I was in the same front room on my own, looking at family photographs and becoming very weepy. Again the smell returned in the opposite corner where one of my grandsons often played. I had sensed by this time what was happening and called my Dad's name to let him know I was there. This was the last time the smell appeared. I have often read that loved ones go to a place they knew happiness as they move on to a different sphere.

Marie, County Kilkenny, Ireland

My grandmother died on 15 August 1996 and my heart just broke when it happened. I was with her at the time, as were other members of her family. She died very peacefully in hospital. I was very close to her and really regarded her as my mother as she had reared me since I was a small child.

When she died I cried as I never had before and I just couldn't stop. As a result I ended up with an infection in both tear ducts. I really couldn't cope at all.

Then something so simple and unbelievable happened and I was amazed. When I returned from the church after her removal I was in my bedroom changing my clothes; my family were in another room so no one was in the room with me and I started to cry again, when this smell wafted past me and I just suddenly smiled and said, 'You are still here with me, thanks Nanny.'

She never wore perfume; it was the smell of talc or something similar that I had noticed when she was in the hospital.

The feeling I felt I can't really put into words; all I know is that I had smiled for the first time in three days and such a feeling of peace and contentment came over me and helped me through the funeral the next day.

I have often shed a tear since remembering things and at special times in the family like weddings or christenings. I know from that smell that day that she is still around me and through that experience I felt a bond that still connects me to her.

I never told anyone of this experience. About three weeks later I was in town collecting a photograph of Nanny that I had had enlarged and framed. It was the last photo I had ever taken of her. It was on her birthday on June 2nd. My eldest daughter was with me and as we chatted I felt I should tell her that I had something kind of strange to say about something that had happened after Nanny was brought to the church.

With that, before I had said another word, she said the word 'smell': I nearly crashed the car! It turned out she had exactly the same experience as me the same night. She too had felt so comforted but a bit strange and was going to tell me at some stage when she had plucked up the courage to.

She was so pleased to know that we both had shared such a special sense and when she had her experience she was twenty miles away in another house and neither of us knew until we were talking that day about Nanny.

My daughter was nineteen years old at the time.

7

Coincidence

The definition of a coincidence is 'a chance occurrence of events remarkable either for being simultaneous or for apparently being connected'. Testimonies in this chapter tell of events too poignantly related to deceased loved ones to simply be coincidences.

Our first testimony from Ann in County Leitrim sets the scene for those that follow in this chapter. After the death of her mother, Ann was devastated to learn that her mother's wedding ring had been lost by the hospital. Curiously, however, soon after an exact replica of this ring found its way to her in a peculiar way.

In this chapter we hear from other people who have experienced such puzzling events and have been left wondering if they have in fact received a message from the afterlife.

Ann, County Leitrim, Ireland

It's almost twenty years since my mother passed away unexpectedly after routine surgery, which was a tremendous shock and upset to us all.

When I collected my mother's personal belongings from the hospital I noticed that her wedding ring was missing. My mother had just one ring, her wedding ring as she had never had an engagement ring. Hospital staff checked thoroughly for the ring but to no avail sadly.

As I am the only daughter I always expected to inherit my mother's wedding ring.

I was absolutely devastated that the ring was missing as it would have been a reassurance to me to wear my mother's ring as she had never taken it off her finger since her marriage in the later forties. I prayed really hard and did novenas that I might get word from the hospital that the ring had been found but all to no avail.

Three months passed and still no sign of the ring. Towards the end of September I purchased a Halloween brac in my local supermarket. When cutting the brac I found, wrapped in a piece of paper, an announcement that I had won a gold ring. All I had to do was send the paper back to the bakery complete with my details.

About a week later my ring was delivered. As I opened up the box and peeled away the tissue paper layer by layer, I could scarcely believe my eyes! There nestling in the box lay the exact replica of my mother's ring! With my heart racing I took the ring from the box and slipped it on my finger.

A feeling of sheer joy washed all over me. I knew in my heart that my mother had sent me a message to reassure me. The ring had a very narrow band, exactly as my mother's ring had been, as was the style in the late 1940s when my parents had married.

I truly believe that the ring which I won and now wear on my finger was sent to replace my mother's lost ring, as my mother was a very selfless woman who would do anything for her family, friends and neighbours.

I believe that she was aware of my deep upset at not having her ring, that she sent me an exact replica of it so that I would be aware that she was continuing to look after me and all the family.

Mary, Manchester, UK

My husband passed away recently. We used to go and visit my mother who lives near Blackpool every Thursday. I would take her shopping and arrive back at the house in time for lunch, leaving my husband to watch television.

A couple of months later – and this has happened twice – the phone has rung at my mother's house. I answered it one time, the line was open, meaning there was someone there. I could sense it as well, but no one spoke. I put the phone down, dialled 1471 to recall the telephone number. The call wasn't registered!

As I said this happened twice and both times on a Thursday after we arrived back after shopping.

Tom, County Westmeath, Ireland

My name is Tom. I was brought up in County Roscommon on a farm. My first experience was when I was ten years old.

My grandfather on my mother's side had been an invalid for some years. When my mother and I used to visit him we would ask him how he was and he would say he was 'not too bad'. In the summer he loved to be out in the wheelchair listening to hear the cuckoo. In the winter he would say, 'I don't mind so long as I live to see the cuckoo.'

A strange thing happened on the night he was waked. It was in the month of May. There was a very large window in the room where he was laid out. In the garden in front of the window was a tree.

All the neighbours gathered that night for the wake and who should come and perch in the tree in front of the window only the cuckoo! He sang there all night until day break and then he disappeared.

The neighbours said 'Will somebody go out and hunt that cuckoo away!' but nobody did. If it was during the day you would not mind so much but to come in the dark of night a cuckoo at a wake seemed very strange! Who sent the cuckoo and how did he know where to go? There must be some link between them. We will never know.

In the early fifties I went to England where I worked in different towns. I took an apartment in a big Victorian building. There were four apartments altogether in the building and a kitchen and living room on the ground floor. The two bedrooms were on the first floor. There was a cellar off the kitchen. When I moved in I went down into the cellar to have a look around. There were three rows of shelves all around the wall. There was everything there you could imagine – books, umbrellas, prams, bicycles.

After having a good look around I walked over to the bookshelf and took out a book. When I opened the book what did I see but a ten thousand mark note! Just then my hair started to rise and I sensed that there was somebody beside me. I left the book back on the shelf and went back to the kitchen where I paced up and down wondering what was there. After a few minutes I decided I was not going to be put off. I went back down again and this time I brought the book back with me.

Some days after I was having tea in the kitchen. It was a lovely sunny day when all of a sudden the kitchen went dark and my hair started to curl. I could feel the presence of someone in the room. It passed off after a few minutes. The stairs were in the middle of the building. It was a wooden stairs and you could hear the footsteps of the other residents going up and down.

Some weeks later I became curious when I heard heavy footsteps coming up the stairs at the same time every night. What made me wonder was that it happened at the same time every night, 11 p.m. I decided I would investigate.

This night coming up to 11 p.m. I stood behind the door and just then the footsteps started coming. I caught hold of the door handle ready to open it. As soon as the footsteps stopped I opened the door at once – there was nobody there!

I never went back to the cellar anymore. This building was situated in Manchester. I got married sometime after that and bought a house.

As to how the ten thousand German mark note came to be there, I don't know. I was telling some friends of mine and a priest and the only thing we could think of was whoever the note belonged to, their spirit must have been keeping watching over it. The note itself was not worth anything as it was printed before the war.

8

Feeling of Comfort

This chapter deals with a very common theme in stories of after-death communication, the feelings of solace and comfort gained by those in grief through contact from deceased friends and family members. We hear first a very moving story from Sandra in County Westmeath who lost her baby son just three months into her pregnancy; she believes he has contacted her since his passing, telling her not to forget him and to include him in family life.

Sandra, County Westmeath, Ireland
I have had experiences since I had a miscarriage four years ago. I believe I have been contacted by the son I lost at only three months pregnancy. I am quite sensitive and have gone to a couple of mediums who have confirmed this and advised me to take steps to enhance and develop it. I do believe in the paranormal completely.

I was sitting in my living room watching television on my own. It was late. My attention was drawn to the closed curtains at the other side of the room. At that, the edge of one side lifted up slowly, about quarter way up (full length curtains to the ground). It was held there, for about six or eight seconds. Then they came very slowly down.

No windows were open; there was no wind and no animals around. It struck me it was like something a small child would do, looking to see *what's behind here?*

One morning I was in bed on my own. I was awake. I felt a hand grab a fistful of hair at the back of my head. It was tugged, hard; hard enough to yank back my head. I half sat up and turned round. I knew there was no one there. It was like someone saying 'get up will you?'

I regularly get my back tickled, just below my right shoulder usually, pins and needles. I feel this is to tell me a spirit is round me, could it be my son or my grandfather who I never met but have always believed are there protecting me? My grandfather died a year before I was born. I was the first grandchild; my father and he were not speaking at the time. There was lots of unfinished business.

My son is still around. I get the 'tickling' usually in the kitchen. A medium happened to say that my grandfather visits me when I'm alone in my kitchen. A shadow can be seen there in the corner.

The strangest thing was yet to come. I was in the kitchen doing dishes late one night. I have two small daughters. I was washing the top of a high chair at the sink. It was very dirty so I was scrubbing for some time with my back to the high chair behind me. It had a makeshift cushion on it – really folded up edging to a cot which has long ties/strings out of it. I turned around to put the clean top on the high chair. When I turned, I saw 4 ties/strings that were dangling down, spin and rotate in mid-air. They were off in different directions, some spinning faster than others. It struck me that it was like something a small child would do, twirl strings around the finger and play with these strings.

I stood there for some time watching this, trying not to freak out. There were no doors open, no wind, no explanations. I walked over, shook the material and quickly walked out the kitchen.

My daughter Georgia is now one and a half years old. When she was a new baby I had another experience. She was maybe eight weeks old. I was in a room on my own with her. She was on my lap, feet touching my belly, head at my knees. I was holding her up slightly looking at her. At that, she looked right above my head. She had that look in her eyes that you have when you're looking straight at someone.

She smiled her first big smile.

It was as if she was smiling at someone looking at her right above my head. At the very same moment of this smile I felt the strongest tickling on the top of my head. It scared me. I felt she was looking at someone and that someone was making itself known to me too.

One day I visited my grandfather's grave and put flowers on from my granny's house across the road. I used to always do this when I was younger. I used to sit at the grave and talk to him as if he was there.

A medium told me, 'You don't put flowers on the grave anymore, he misses this. You will again.' That night after putting the flowers on, I was doing the dishes and I got the strongest pins in my back. I knew it was him.

Later I walked out the kitchen. I stopped and came back. I said a few words, 'I know you are here, I know you liked that I put the flowers there, thanks for being round me protecting me, I do need you and will not forget you.'

At that, I heard footsteps on the wooden floor behind me. Maybe six steps or so, very clear, walking across the floor.

I haven't had any activity in some time. I am very busy with work and with my two little children. I suppose it happens when I'm more open to it. I did get tickles in the back a couple of times when, as a family, we were out to dinner. I believe it was Francis my son saying, 'I'm here too, don't forget to include me in the family meals out.'

Mary, County Roscommon, Ireland

I was born in Northern Ireland but in August 2001 I was living with my husband and two children in Roscommon. My marriage was at breaking point and so too was my sanity. I was suffering from post-traumatic stress due to the Troubles and surviving with the effects on a day-to-day basis.

On Saturday August 18th my oldest nephew, Gary, was killed in a motorcycle accident in New York. He was born when I was living out of the country and even though I loved him, I can't say I was very close to him, certainly not in comparison with other members of my family.

That night I cried my eyes out, for a lost life, a young life, but also for myself. The following day I took to the hills, walking with friends so that I could find peace. At that time the mountains were the only place I found it and I felt him with me, I just knew it was him and he told me he would be there for me.

Shocked, I thought no more about it but I felt a comfort and a strength around me that I had not had before. I began to carry his picture with me and when the pain of long forgotten memories would surface I would hold that picture to my heart as I cried.

Six months later my husband and I parted and I began my own healing process which was a slow painful journey back to myself

Once when I was much better I asked Gary – I was now talking to him whenever I needed to – 'Why did you contact me?'

He answered, 'I knew if I helped you, you would help the rest of them.' I assumed by saying 'the rest of them' he was referring to the rest of the family.

I continued the healing process through my meditations and sought therapy and counselling when needed, also helping my younger sister to do the same.

About six years after his death I had to face the most horrific memory that I thought I would never have the courage to face. I cut all contact with my friends and therapists to do this as I could no longer verbalise it.

For over six months I was mostly alone, my children now at college. I faced it, bit by bit, day after day with Gary at my side (morning, noon and night). When the worst was over I knew I could forgive, let go and move on.

During this time I wrote the most disturbing things that arose from the memories and burnt them all months later when the process was finished and I was ready to let go.

A few weeks later, knowing that I could now move on, I was deciding what to do with my future as my children were only home at weekends and I was free. I turned on the radio to listen to the late Gerry Ryan one Monday morning at the beginning of 2009.

When I realised he was not on air, I was about to turn it off when a lady said if you ever thought of writing a book stay tuned. I had thought of writing, as people were always telling me that I should write a book. But when the author she was interviewing said, two thousand words a chapter, one hundred thousand words for a book I laughed and was about to turn the radio off when I heard her say it took her two months to write the first two thousand words.

Something in me immediately knew this is what I was meant to do even though I had never had any intentions of writing a book, had no idea how one started and English was the only subject that I had ever failed! I turned off the radio and on the computer.

Three hours later I had two thousand words written and the story was flowing. Before the night was out I had four thousand words and I knew two things and both of them frightened me.

One was that I would finish the book and two that it would be published.

Two weeks later I had seventy thousand words in front of me, a few days after that when the initial shock of what I had written had worn off, I started from the beginning and began correcting it.

I had nothing but positive comments from people who read it for me. After being professionally edited, it was then endorsed by the best selling historic novelist, Morgan Llywelyn and there was no problem getting a publisher.

It was on the shelves nine years after Gary's death and I believe he was with me every step of the way. I also believe the book will help people who have been traumatised, by whatever means, by finding that trust within themselves, facing and acknowledging what happened to them, forgiving whoever they need to and moving on to a brighter future; I have with the help of my nephew who knew only too well the effects the war had on children.

The name of the book is *The Long Road Home*.

Phil, County Kildare, Ireland

My husband died suddenly in December 2000, leaving me with three children to bring up on my own. As you can appreciate we were all a bit shell-shocked at how quickly our lives had changed. He was buried on 15 December so Christmas was a bit of a blur. In 2001 my youngest son made his communion and my oldest sat his Junior Cert. As a family we always had a family holiday every year but I found I just couldn't bring myself to book one. I was nervous of going abroad with three children on my own. However, I felt they needed a break as they had a hard year too, so on the spur of the moment I visited the local travel agent.

I booked a holiday in Turkey, not by choice but because it was the only place available. We headed off to Alayna in Turkey and booked in to our hotel.

Downstairs at the reception there was bookshelves with books you could take to read and you could leave maybe a book you had taken on holidays to read and were finished with.

One day I was passing and saw an Irish Independent newspaper. I love reading newspapers and especially the Independent. I opened the paper to read it and found it was the edition from 14 December 2000 – the one that contained my husband Peter's death notice. This particular hotel did not have many Irish guests and that was the only Irish paper I saw on my travels. I felt it was Peter's way of telling us he was watching over us.

Incidentally on the second week a couple who my husband knew well turned up in the same hotel. They found themselves there as it was the only place available. They had been away when Peter died and had been unable to attend his funeral and I had not seen them since his death.

9

Miscellaneous

The stories in this section are diverse and varied and did not fit into any of the other chapters so have been given a category of their own. We hear stories of loss and contact; and we hear a very moving story from Galway about a mother who believes her late father was there to welcome her teenage daughter in heaven after she had died tragically. 'The feeling I got from my dad was one of comfort and not of being scared and I knew that he would look after her,' writes a comforted Bernadette.

Linda, Ontario, Canada

I have always been a spiritual person, believing in a better place and an afterlife, angels and the greater power of the universe and God.

My mom was a wonderful lady and when she became palliative I was her caregiver.

One night she told me there were people in the house – she described them. The veil had lifted, I knew. Although she straddled the fence when it came to believing what I believed I would talk to her often of the beautiful place she would go to where there would be no more pain and she would be dancing on fields of wild flowers.

She would smile that smile that asked 'Do you think so?' I pleaded with her to give me a sign after she was gone, a sign to tell me she was ok and that I was right. I said, 'Mom, it has to be right in my face. I don't want to miss it and question it.'

She passed away on 30 May 2010. About a month or so later I was sitting outside on a bright sunny morning looking out at the garden when this beautiful butterfly sat on my knee. I was mesmerised as it sat there for what seemed like quite a while. Suddenly, it flew up into my face. I could feel its wings fluttering on my cheek. What a wonderful sign! I now have a monarch butterfly tattooed above my heart.

Patricia, Lancashire, UK

I'm a great believer in some form of afterlife. I lost my husband twenty years ago. We had always talked about a 'heaven' or such like and he promised me if that if it were possible he would let me know about it.

About six months after he died I was in bed asleep when I saw lots of blue flashing lights. I was really scared thinking it was a police incident or something similar. Then I felt his hands on my shoulders. Again I was really afraid, and then I heard my husband's voice. His words were, 'Don't be afraid, I'll always be there for you.' The incident was brief but so clear and from that day on I felt peaceful, more so I think because I believed then that one day we would be reunited.

The second incident was more painful to me. I lost one of my grandsons very suddenly and for no apparent reason. Gary was only twenty-five years of age. He had never had any illness but the day he died he came home from work feeling unwell. He played some games with his younger brother, and then he said he felt tired. He lay down on the sofa and just went to sleep.

It was never discovered why he died and all that they could tell us was that it was like an adult cot death. To say we were all devastated was a light way of putting it. I tried to be brave because of my daughter's grief and that of the rest of the family.

Several weeks passed by and I know once again I had gone to sleep weeping. Gary had been so close to me. Then I was suddenly on a street in an area I did not know. There were crowds of people lining the streets. One of them was a young lady Carol who I know was a friend of my daughter. I said, 'What's going on Carol?'

She burst out laughing and said, 'It's a charity run and guess what? We are waiting for your Gary!' It was a standing joke in the family that Gary was always late. However, a taxi pulled in at that point and out jumped four young men. Gary was one of them.

I stood there, tears in my eyes. He came forward and said, 'Yo Nanna, give me a kiss and a hug.' Then he said he had to go and set off on the run with the rest. I woke up crying and wished that I could say the event had given me some sense of peace but I felt it was his last goodbye because he had not been able to say this to anyone and I also felt it was some sign that he still needed me.

He left behind a baby son Owen who is now four and we speak about his daddy to him often. He thinks his daddy is a star in the sky and often when they are there to be seen he speaks to his daddy. I have not really found any reason for either of these events. They are still as fresh in my mind as when they occurred so I believe in what I saw and heard.

Maeve, County Dublin, Ireland
The first event I can really remember was a friend of mine who sadly passed away in tragic circumstances. Before anybody informed me of his passing I knew myself that he was gone. It was a very strong feeling of loss inside of me although I didn't really know at that point who I was going to hear had passed away.

I was working in Dublin at the time and had taken the day off work as I knew there was going to be a knock on my door some time that day. My sister had taken the train to Dublin to tell me my friend had passed away and when I opened the door to her, I looked at her face and I knew then who it was so I just said, 'I know.'

We travelled home and after the funeral I returned to Dublin. I could feel his presence with me when I was alone in my room. It was a feeling of knowing someone was there, almost like their presence carried an invisible weight.

Often when I would be upset in grief, I would be lying down on my bed and my body would be shaking in my sobbing when his presence would manifest itself as a weight on top of me and a calmness would come over me and I would stop crying, breathe evenly, calm down and drift into a peaceful sleep.

I became so aware of him being in my room that I would just speak to him from time to time just like normal. It was never anything but comfortable. He brought me great peace when I needed it. His presence was there in the background right up to the time I moved out. This was about eighteen years ago and still to this day if I am alone driving along in the car he may pop into my head and within minutes a song will come on the radio that he would sing or a mutual friend will phone me and I know it's him saying hello.

I also had an experience when I was in my great-uncle's house one day. This was an old house that had not been lived in for several years. After struggling to get the front door open as it had seized up I went into the house. The layout was very simple a very long corridor with four door off it and leading to a back kitchen. Three of the rooms were bedrooms and one a kitchen cum living room with a big open fire and chain to hang a pot on. The bedrooms were all damp with the ceiling falling down in some of them and one wall in the kitchen/dining room was all dampness and the house smelt of mould and damp.

Once I went out to the back kitchen I was hit by the sweetest smell. It was like someone had just sprayed a floral air freshener but yet it wasn't. I couldn't recognise the smell at all. It was the sweetest, most vibrant, awaking smell ever and it stayed in my nostrils for a long time.

There was nobody in the house with me so I just acknowledged that it belonged to either my great-uncle or his wife as they had no children so I just spoke and told them stuff like my father was fine, I hoped they were fine. It was again comfortable, just like I walked in and they didn't expect me, like I'd caught them off guard.

Another experience occurred less than a year ago. I was in bed alone when I felt a presence in the room. I knew someone would be there when I opened my eyes. I sat up in the bed and at the foot of my bed stood a man. I wasn't afraid of him or anything I felt he was no threat to me.

He said, 'Do you know who I am?'

I said, 'Yes, you are —.'

He said, 'Don't be afraid.'

I said, 'I'm not.' I asked him if he wanted to say a prayer and I started to say the Hail Mary out loud and some time before I finished he had disappeared. The unusual thing about this visit was that it was the first time I could see the person. Also the man was known to me but only an acquaintance.

He would come into the restaurant where I worked once a week for lunch with two other men. His first name I knew so well but not his surname, before that night you could have offered me a million pounds to remember it and I would not have been able to but when he asked it slipped off my tongue like a song.

Also the last time I would have seen this man would have been ten years ago at least and I think he died about seven years ago. The last time I would have thought about him would have been two maybe three years before that when I saw one of the other men he worked with and he came to my mind. I didn't know he died until sometime after it had happened. Also, I prayed with him but it's not something I do. I don't go to Mass but I did mention in passing to members of my family who go to mass to say a prayer there for him as I think he may have been asking for that.

My family don't question me when I tell them of my various experiences they are so used to it now. As a small child I always spoke to and of people no one else could see, or told of dreams I had that would come true – good and bad. I didn't like this so I mentally closed this part of my mind shut and haven't opened it since. He didn't scare me I just went back to sleep again.

Bernadette, County Galway, Ireland
My sixteen year old daughter had been raped in 2001. My dad had passed away six months before that and my mother had said to go down to the graveyard and as I walked down it suddenly struck me to hide my tablets. It came into my head and then it went out of my head again. My daughter was very down and we had had a few words over nothing and she had gone into her bedroom. At half five that evening my sister had called for a cup of tea and she went off home.

I was washing up my cup and this beautiful wonderful feeling came over me and I could feel it creeping up on me and I knew it was my dad. This warm gentle breeze engulfed me and I remember saying to him 'Jesus Dad, thanks a million for calling!' So at that the gentle breeze went off my cheeks and I remember thinking *well if that's heaven I wouldn't mind being there! It was very very comforting.*

At about half eight that evening my daughter, who was just sixteen years of age, committed suicide. Someone was warning me but I don't know who. She passed away and they couldn't save her. But the feeling I got from my dad was one of comfort and not of being scared and I knew that he would look after her.

After my daughter died I got a beautiful smell of flowers three times. Little things have happened and I know she is there. I bring my father's cardigan and her jumper to bed every night and once I got up in the morning and on the floor was my dad's cardigan and my daughter's jumper with her sleeve in his sleeve neatly on the floor – and it's like they're together now. I feel my daughter is very happy now.

M. McGilloway, UK

My story begins in the mid sixties when I was living with my family in Aberdeen Scotland. My wife, who is a believer, had just given birth to our third and youngest son Keith who had an intolerance to sugar in his bottled feed. Consequently any food that he consumed was after a few minutes, rejected by his stomach. Therefore he was losing weight rapidly. He was admitted to the local hospital and the nursing sister asked the local priest to attend our son and he administered the last rights.

Our son's frail body would not stabilise and we were summoned to his bedside on several occasions but eventually he started to gain weight. We decided as a family to go on holiday to my parent's house in Derry.

A few days after we arrived my mother suggested that my wife and I visit my sister who lived a few miles away. When we returned about two hours later my mother was settling by the fire and we asked her if Keith was alright and she told us what happened. She was downstairs in the kitchen when she heard my father's voice calling her. When there was something that was frustrating him he called my mother by her maiden name: 'Mary Doherty, this child here is crying.' My mother went upstairs and found Keith upstairs in the room next to my father's. My mother found the child drowning in his own vomit.

We rushed downstairs and summoned an ambulance which rushed Keith to the nearest hospital. When we arrived back my mother was sat trembling by the dying fire because she realised that my father had died about ten years previously. Keith is now a healthy man approaching fifty years old.

Eileen, Surrey, UK

I would like to tell you of my two small experiences. I am now seventy-seven years old and my experiences were at the age of eleven and again when I was twenty-four.

Aged eleven I lived with an aunt of mine in a flat over her hairdressing business in Exetor, Devon. In the lounge was a photo of a very handsome man aged twenty. He was Pilot Philip Clements, a neighbour and friend of my grandmother who lived in a quaint Devon village.

One afternoon I came home from school and on going up to the flat I looked at Philip's photo and knew he had died. I just stood there. My aunt came upstairs and put her arms around me and said 'I have bad news, Philip's plane has crashed and he has been killed' but I already somehow knew. It was 1944.

The second experience was in 1957 and happened in quite a different way. It was April and my father was seriously ill. He had always hoped to have a son but there was only my sister and myself. My sister had two girls at that time but my first born was a boy Liam. My father was ecstatic!

Liam was two years old and my daughter six months old when Dad became seriously ill. This particular night I was sitting up in bed saying the rosary when I fell asleep. It was a very short time later when I became alert to a rushing sort of wind which flew up the stairs into the bedroom where I was with my babies and straight to Liam's cot, but not to me and not to baby Susan. It was nine o'clock in the evening. I was curious but not afraid and went back to sleep.

A neighbour, who had a phone, woke me at seven o'clock the next morning to tell me my father had passed away at nine o'clock the previous evening. I am certain his spirit came immediately to see this precious grandchild whom he hadn't seen for six months as we were living in Dublin and on coming home to England to be with him during his surgery, Liam had not been allowed into the hospital.

Carl, USA

My maternal grandfather passed away when I was seven. We were fairly close. The morning he died, before we got the call, my mother said she saw a shooting star when taking out the trash. Later when we found out the exact time of death, the two events coincided. Shortly after he passed, my mother and I went to a grocery store near his house, the same one he always went to.

We got out of the car and started toward the front doors. A man came out carrying a brown bag of groceries. Immediately I recognised him. He looked just like my grandfather! He stared straight at me as he passed us and winked on his way by. I turned to my mom but she was rummaging in her purse and didn't appear to have seen him. I quickly told her to look, saying that the man looked like grandpa. But when we turned to look, he was gone. No cars were around but ours and no cars were starting up or leaving. The gentleman had just vanished!

Nothing else happened until I was about twelve years of age. My maternal grandmother passed away and we had to clean out the house. One of the things we brought back were two old hand-coloured portraits of my grandparents that had sat on display in the old house. They were important to them and my mom said they'd been displayed since she was a kid. She let me have them in my room and I put them proudly on a shelf with other family pictures. That's when things started happening.

The most vivid memory was when I was blasting my stereo really loud one day. No one else was home and I was listening to Metallica, which I knew my mother would not approve of, at least not at the volume I had it!

I was painting, in my own world when all of a sudden one of my brushes flew off my desk and across the room, hitting the wooden frame of the bed and bouncing off it. There was a lot of force behind it! At the same time my stereo turned off too. I didn't know what to think at first. It was a little too real if you get my meaning.

It dawned on me fairly quickly though what was happening, so I looked up at the portrait of my grandfather and said, 'Ok Grandpa, I'll turn it down. How about I listen to something else?' Nothing else happened that day, in fact as soon as I put on something a little more respectful the air in the room got lighter and my anxiety disappeared.

All through high school it was like that. If I was watching something on TV that was inappropriate the TV would turn off. Or if my brother was being a bully, and we were yelling, doors would slam. I know my brother had experiences on his own, but to this day he won't tell me about them.

When I was eighteen I left home to live with my father in Maine. I took the portraits with me, but then accidentally left them in a drawer when I moved back home. Sometimes I want them back, and I know my dad would send them. But I'm not sure I want those things to happen again. I have my own children now, and they may not understand. I don't want them being afraid in their own house.

Joshua, USA

One night, 30 October 2000, at 1.32 a.m., I woke up from a dead sleep. I didn't know why I woke up but had the feeling of warmth and comfort, something important had happened and I didn't know what it was. I turned on my light in my bedroom and looked around; there was nothing unusual in my room, nothing out of the ordinary. Yet I still had that feeling like the warmth and love you feel spending time with someone important in your life. I decided that I would go back to sleep and tell my parents in the morning. When I woke the next morning I went downstairs to get breakfast.

As I was sitting at the table my parents had got up and made coffee. As we were sitting there eating breakfast, I told my mom that I had woke and had a strange feeling like warmth of love and it startled me because I was not sure what was doing it. I never woke up like that before, feeling like I just had a conversation and was going to say goodbye. After I had explained the event that took place, she told me at 1.30 a.m. my grandmother had died in her sleep at the hospital.

I didn't even know she was in the hospital! That really made me feel creeped out. My mom has always been the one who would tell you who was calling before the phone rang, and other weird oddities as well. She is no psychic but she told me she had woken up that night also and said it was my grandmother saying goodbye. I really miss her; she was a pivotal part of all our lives.

I apologise if I am not a great storyteller, but I have been in the Marine Corps now for ten years and think about that night quite often; it is a reminder that one day

I will see her again, as well as a reassurance that I will be able to say goodbye to my loved ones when the time comes.

Margaret, Ireland

I used to work in London doing office and house cleaning. One particular place where we worked was a shop with two flats overhead. A mother, aged eighty-three, lived in one and her daughter aged sixty lived in the top one. They had a cat called Sophie who had the run of the building from the top flat to the basement. This was an indoor cat who never went out, probably because there was a very busy road outside.

We went there every week to clean and we also did the shopping. The basement was a converted cat museum with almost everything devoted to cats, even the curtains. The shop was full of antiques but the cat was allowed to sit wherever she wanted.

One day we were asked by the daughter if we would witness her and her mothers wills, which we did.

The daughter asked us to help her move all her books from the shelves in her top floor flat because she was getting the painter in. This room contained a lot of books and it was a very long process taking down all the books. It took a whole afternoon and we were all tired afterwards. Subsequently the painter came and did his job and then we put all the books back where they were before.

One morning afterwards I was going past the building and saw the police outside and wondered what was going on. I went in and up to the mother's flat only to be told that her daughter was dead. She had committed suicide which she had planned for some time. She had left a note asking if we would take the cat Sophie (she knew we also had cats).

We collected Sophie in the cat basket and took her home. We lived in a three bedroom house with two reception rooms downstairs. The back room was where we left Sophie when we went upstairs to bed that night. The front sitting room had book shelves both sides of the chimney breast. On one of the top shelves was a heavy book which lay flat, was not as wide as the shelf and had been there for years. The shelf was solid and secure.

On the lower shelves was a mixture of books and ornaments. The door to the room was closed. During the night we heard a crash and when I went in and looked, the book was lying on the floor. It came from the top shelf but nothing was broken. It was as if it was picked up and thrown down. Nothing else was touched and no ornaments broken!

How this happened I have no idea because there was no way that book would have fallen off the shelf – so, you know what I was thinking! I don't really have any belief in any of that sort of thing but yet I can't dismiss what happened and there has to be a connection.

A couple of weeks later it was December and Christmas was coming up when there was a knock on the door and a hamper was delivered from the person who had died. This was a nice deep basket that when emptied was ideal for a cat to sleep in. Although this happened twelve years ago we still have the basket. Skippy, one of our cats likes to sleep in it.

The mother died less than a month after the daughter; the shock killed her. Sophie came with us to Ireland but by then she was old and she died after a couple of years. This is a very sad story and a shocking one because we found out later that the daughter had MS and couldn't face the prospect of life in a wheelchair.

I haven't mentioned any names because I don't think it would be fair on the people but this is a true story. We still think of them every time we look at the basket.

Afterword

As a conclusion I have added an interview conducted with Shane McCorristine, a historian who holds a PhD in the supernatural. McCorristine provides a very interesting and valuable historical perspective on the subject of after-death communication.

Dubliner Shane McCorristine is an interdisciplinary historian with an interest in cultural, social, literary, and environmental history. He focuses on the intangible, the supernatural and the disembodied as expressed and understood in different historical contexts and under different frames of meaning.

Now based in the UK, we spoke about his vast interest in the world of the supernatural and that of after-death communication. His fascination goes back to his childhood: 'I was always interested in reading ghost stories such as those by Bram Stoker. I liked medical theories about why people saw ghosts and then I went on to take a PhD in the subject.'

McCorristine wonders why other historians never saw ghosts as valuable material as he feels there's a value in studying the dreams of the nineteenth-century society and the kind of dreams people were having. Shane says after-death communication was particularly prevalent around the nineteenth century. 'At that time there were changing ideas about death,' he explains, 'and it is very difficult to chart those changes but there was always a continuity in what people thought of as magical imagination.'

Every class has superstitions and traditions but in the nineteenth century what you had was academics and professionals who started to say that certain things were primitive and certain things were pseudoscientific. They spoke of telepathy or thought transferences. Love charms, angels or Marian apparitions became part of something that was non-scientific and Dr McCorristine thinks this is what lead to what we know today as parapsychology.

So, does McCorristine believe that faith in after-death communication brings people comfort or further pain and upset? In some cases, he believes it initially brought confusion. 'I think for a lot of people, especially all the middle class people, they didn't know what to do with it and one of the big things in England was to send your report to the Society for Psychic Research. This was a group of very respectable psychics, lawyers and investigators. They endeavoured to get a critical mass of evidence in order to prove that such things could happen. I think some people did get comfort, but because it was the nineteenth century and because there were new distinctions between popular beliefs and new beliefs, there was a huge emphasis on embarrassment about seeing ghosts. There was also a new distinction about what you thought about the afterlife in that period, not just in the Catholic Church, but in the Anglican Church.'

After-death communication and people's urge to maintain contact with their deceased loved ones is clearly big business and this is where mediums and clairvoyants come in. So what is McCorristine's view on them? Genuine or dangerous?

'I think that many scholars now sidestep the question of whether mediums are authentic or fraudulent, and whether what they say is true or false. I would say that it is arguably more interesting to explore the why, what, and how of mediums and their claims. As long as people die, there will be people who seek or obtain contact with them, however that may be.

'For instance, why are most mediums female, and why do we feel that women (and maybe children) have closer access to spirits than others? Why have people in all cultures and periods in history consulted members of a community who claim different ways of knowing than the rest of us?

'In hunter-gatherer and animistic societies, shamans would provide a crucial function for the community by maintaining a link to the other world, informing the tribe of hunting conditions, and giving accounts of other lands and worlds. In the modern world, mediums still perform essential cultural work. They challenge the idea that life and consciousness are the same thing; they pose questions about the power of the unconscious; they ask us to imagine what an afterlife might look like.'

McCorristine also has specific views on how mediums actually operate. 'All mediums perform and all audiences perform. These performances change depending on what culture and time you are in. In modern UK and Ireland I would suggest that most people who go to seances, or mediumistic performances, have the same mentality as people who go to see a horror movie or go to a political rally: they have a suspension of disbelief, they let themselves, for a period, be drawn in by an atmosphere, and questions of whether this is true or false only come after. For many mediums it is probably the same process. So taken together, these questions make mediums and psychics part of what it means to be human.'

All the people in this book have diverse and very interesting views. As a journalist I remain objective, make no judgements and respectfully allow the eye-witness accounts speak for themselves. If you have had an experience relating to contact and it has brought you comfort then I believe that that is the only thing that matters.

I hope you will draw further reassurance and empathy from the other people's stories in this compilation.